How to Listen to a Gemini

Real Life Guidance on How to Get Along and
Be Friends with the 3rd Sign of the Zodiac

How to Listen to a Gemini

Real Life Guidance on How to Get Along and
Be Friends with the 3rd Sign of the Zodiac

Mary L. English

Winchester, UK
Washington, USA

First published by Dodona Books, 2013
Dodona Books is an imprint of John Hunt Publishing Ltd., Laurel House, Station Approach,
Alresford, Hants, SO24 9JH, UK
office1@jhpbooks.net
www.johnhuntpublishing.com
www.dodona-books.com

For distributor details and how to order please visit the 'Ordering' section on our website.

Text copyright: Mary L. English 2013

ISBN: 978 1 78279 099 0

All rights reserved. Except for brief quotations in critical articles or reviews, no part of this
book may be reproduced in any manner without prior written permission from the publishers.

The rights of Mary L. English as author have been asserted in accordance with the Copyright,
Designs and Patents Act 1988.

A CIP catalogue record for this book is available from the British Library.

Design: Lee Nash

Printed and bound by CPI Group (UK) Ltd, Croydon, CR0 4YY

We operate a distinctive and ethical publishing philosophy in all
areas of our business, from our global network of authors to
production and worldwide distribution.

CONTENTS

Also by Mary English

6 Easy Steps in Astrology
The Birth Charts of Indigo Children
How to Survive a Pisces (O-Books)
How to Bond with an Aquarius (O-Books)
How to Cheer Up a Capricorn (O-Books)
How to Believe in a Sagittarius (O-Books)
How to Win the Trust of a Scorpio (Dodona Books)
How to Love a Libra (Dodona Books)
How to Soothe a Virgo (Dodona Books)
How to Lavish a Leo (Dodona Books)
How to Care for a Cancer (Dodona Books)
How to Satisfy a Taurus (Dodona Books)
How to Appreciate an Aries (Dodona Books)

This book is dedicated to three wonderful Geminis:

My lovely Auntie Jo Morgan
(May she rest in peace in heaven),

Oksana for her help with editing and critiquing this series,
and

My best friend Laura who has always encouraged and
supported me.

Acknowledgements

I would like to thank the following people:

My son for being the Libran that makes me always look on the other side.

My Taurus husband Jonathan for being the most wonderful man in the world.

Mabel, Jessica and Usha for their Homeopathic help and understanding.

Mandy for her friendship.

Donna Cunningham for her help and advice.

Judy Hall for her inspiration.

Alois Treindl for being the Pisces that founded the wonderful Astro.com website.

Judy Ramsell Howard at the Bach Centre for her encouragement.

John my publisher for being the person that fought tooth and nail to get this book published, and all the staff at O-Books including Stuart, Trevor, Kate, Nick, Krystina, Catherine, Maria, Elizabeth and Mary.

Victoria, Oksana, Ursula, Mary and Alam for their welcome editing eyes.

And last but not least my lovely clients for their valued contributions.

Introduction

Why the title of this book?

This book is part of a series of Sun sign books, written to help you understand the people in your life. I started at the end of the Zodiac, with *How to Survive a Pisces*, because I am one and I went backwards through the Zodiac. I'm now on my 10th book, about the 3rd sign. Confused? Imagine what it must be like to be me!

I started this book one wild and windy autumn day, with the wind whistling down the chimney in my office and the rain bashing against the front of the house. Not exactly positive weather. After a few moments, the rain moved away and the Sun came out. This is similar to the energies of Gemini. The Twins. The positive and the negative, the good and the bad, the happy and the sad... Gemini has them both.

That's what we need to do when we learn Astrology.

First we learn about ourselves, then we learn about the people nearest to us, then when our confidence grows, we learn about the wider population.

To understand a little better about how Astrology got to where it is today, it helps to learn a bit about its history.

A Brief History of Astrology

Christopher McIntosh, a historian, tells us in his *The Astrologers and Their Creed* that Astrology was discovered in what is now called the Middle East, Iraq:

> It was the priests of the kingdom of Babylonia who made the discovery, which set the pattern for the development of astronomy and of the zodiacal system of astrology that we know today. For many generations they had been meticulously observing and recording the movements of the heavenly bodies. Finally they had, by careful calculation,

discovered that there were, besides the Sun and the Moon, five other visible planets which moved in established courses through the sky. These were the planets that we now call Mercury, Venus, Mars, Jupiter and Saturn.

The discovery which these priest-astronomers made was a remarkable one, considering how crude were the instruments with which they worked. They had no telescopes, nor any of the complicated apparatus, which astronomers use today. But they did have one big advantage. The area, next to the Persian Gulf, on which their kingdom lay, was blessed with extremely clear skies. In order to make full use of this advantage they built towers on flat areas of country and from these were able to scan the entire horizon.

These priests lived highly secluded lives in monasteries usually adjacent to the towers. Every day they observed the movements of the heavenly spheres and noted down any corresponding earthly phenomena from floods to rebellions. Very early on they had come to the conclusion that the laws which governed the movements of the stars and planets also governed events on Earth. The seasons changed with the movements of the Sun, therefore, they argued, the other heavenly bodies must surely exercise a similar influence...

In the beginning the stars and planets were regarded as being actual gods. Later, as religion became more sophisticated, the two ideas were separated and the belief developed that the god 'ruled' the corresponding planet.

Gradually, a highly complex system was built up in which each planet had a particular set of properties ascribed to it. This system was developed partly through the reports of the priests and partly through the natural characteristics of the planets. Mars was seen to be red in colour and was therefore identified with the god Nergal, the fiery god of war and destruction.

Venus, identified by the Sumerians as their goddess

Inanna, was the most prominent in the morning, giving birth, as it were, to the day. She therefore became the planet associated with the female qualities of love, gentleness and reproduction.

The observation of the stars by the Sumerians was mostly a religious act. The planets were their gods and each visible object was associated with an invisible spiritual being that judged their actions, blessed them with good fortune or sent them tribulations.[1]

Astrology was therefore born out of careful observation and also a desire by the Sumerians to add meaning to their lives. At first it was for a practical purpose, to help their crops, and then it developed into one that was spiritual, and thousands of years later Astrology is still with us.

Definition of Astrology

Astrology is the study of the planets but not in the astronomical sense. Astrologers look at the planets and record where they are from the viewpoint of the Earth, and divide the sky into 12 equal portions. Those portions start at the Spring Equinox of 0° Aries. We use astronomical information but the difference between astronomy and Astrology is that Astrologers use this astronomical information for a different purpose. Originally astronomers and Astrologers were the same species, but as science progressed astronomers broke away and focused only on the planets themselves, not on their meaning. Astrologers believe that we are all connected.

As above, so below.

Just as we are all connected as beings from the same human race, Astrologers believe we are all connected in some way to everything around us.

An ongoing activity that Astrologers carry out is to look at the charts of people in the news. I do it all the time and it's fascinating. Why did that person say/do/think that?

And generally we can attribute their behaviour to their Sun sign.

Even someone with only a basic knowledge of Astrology will be able to differentiate between a Leo's sunny character and a Capricorn's more sensible and possibly stern outlook on life.

This is where Sun sign Astrology is so useful. It helps us learn about people's motivations, and if we understand people better, we tend to get along with them better... well that's the plan!

I work in private practice as an Astrologer and Homeopath, seeing clients and patients to help them recover their health, or deal with all sorts of predicaments. I don't see people that are happy or in a good space, and I feel honoured that they choose me to help them. It's a privilege that I am grateful for. I've been 'reading' for clients since I was 13, so over the years I have seen numbers of people. Not all of them have been paying clients. Before I became insured and professional I read for friends and family and people at parties, and at work, on holiday... whenever I was asked. That's how you build up experience, by actually talking with people and finding out 'where they are' in their lives.

I 'became' an Astrologer soon after I trained to be a Homeopath, and it was my Homeopath that set me on the path I am now on, when she said to me something that piqued my curiosity.

I was busy telling her about something that had happened to me when I was in my late 20s. *"Oh, that must have been during your Saturn Return,"* she said. *"Saturn Return,"* I thought. *"What the heck is **that?**"*

I didn't like to ask her because she's a Homeopath, not an Astrologer, but I set off to investigate what she was on about. And I read lots of books, made lots of charts for my friends and family... and spent a number of years teaching myself, at my own pace, so I was absolutely confident when I started to use Astrology in my practice.

I was already using palmistry and card readings, and Astrology seemed to be a nice 'add-on', something that would help me understand my clients better.

What I didn't realise at that time was how much of my life would be taken up with that study and how fascinating the whole subject would be... and still is.

I don't see how you can tire of Astrology...

Anyway.

I learned from the writings of wonderful Astrologers such as Judy Hall and Donna Cunningham. I joined the Astrological Association of Great Britain and wrote my own newsletter, which I e-mailed to clients or visitors to my website, and threw myself *totally* into the subject.

The first thing I learned was I had something called a Leo Ascendant. And that explained to me why when I read Sun sign books, like the lovely Linda Goodman's *Sun Signs*, and *Love Signs*, why her descriptions just didn't quite fit.

My auntie, my father's sister, was interested in Astrology and died way before I became seriously interested. Two of my Aquarian sisters were more versed in Astrology than me, so when I started this learning curve everything began to make sense.

The reason I liked my aunt and got on so well with her was because I had a Gemini Moon, and she was a Gemini Sun, so there was a sort of mutual understanding. She also had Moon in Leo and I have a Leo Ascendant, so again there was a match. She never pushed her Astrology on to me, but would occasionally offer to 'do the chart' of a boyfriend and when she died I asked my uncle if I could have her books and he kindly gave me two of her ephemerides, and one of them had my name next to my date of birth.

How cool was that!

When I did the chart of my best friend, someone I have known for years and years and years, we met as teenagers, I discovered this:

I am a Pisces with Moon in Gemini and she is a Gemini with Moon in Pisces! That made such an impact on me.

Why would I keep or be friends with someone for that amount of time?

We've both been married, divorced, then remarried (happily) but we live completely different lives. She works in finance, I work in esoterica. She has a 'regular' job, I work for myself. So you can't say that we met because of work. That would never have happened. In fact, we met because our ex-husbands were friends. And they are now not friends with each other, and we are. We've stuck through thick and thin and I can only put it down to that mutual reception of the Sun/Moon thing.

That's when Astrology becomes *so* meaningful... and we'll learn in this little book about you and your Gemini, and why *they* might be the way they are.

Bath

November 2012

Chapter One

The Sign

Gemini is The Twins. The double-bodied sign of the Zodiac. The other double is Pisces, which is represented by the two fish swimming in opposite directions.

And here is the eternal dilemma... doing one thing, and thinking something else.

Saying one thing and doing something completely different. It's something that all Geminis suffer from, this ability to see two sides to a situation, give two versions of events, and want to know not only the good things in life, but also the worst. My ex-husband, who is a Gemini, used to say he'd never hope for something good, in case he was disappointed, so he'd always think about the worst-case scenario.

Not sure if it works, or if he still thinks like that, but it was something he told me.

Here's Peter, an administrative assistant and part-time software writer. I asked him how he first got into Astrology and he gave me some good reasons for feeling at home with the descriptions that his Sun sign is supposed to have:

I'm a Sun in Gemini. But when I read about Sun in Gemini, I thought, "Yes! This is me!" but underneath it was a sense of actually is this REALLY me or do I just really relate or resonate with this because I WANT it to be? And I think it's a bit of both. I don't think I'm actually as amazing as Gemini sounded when I read it, but I really wanted to be and I really came away feeling upbeat and positive that I could do anything and be the best version of myself that I could be, but I wasn't really there yet. I really felt that Sun in Gemini must be the very best Sun sign around. As a control I read Sun in Aries as I was skeptical that maybe they all relate to you and they're written in a vague way that applies to all. But it wasn't. I didn't relate to it at all.

Later I went and bought the book (I was a student and prior to this I was just sneakily reading it in a bookshop) and I read the whole thing straight through. Some of the other signs really resonated with me, particularly Aquarius, Scorpio and parts of Libra. I have nothing in Libra, but I later discovered that I also had something called an Ascendant in Scorpio, whatever on earth that was, and that other planets counted too, such as the Moon, which was in Aquarius.

So what is a Gemini?

To call someone a Gemini, they would need to be born between a certain set of dates. These are the ones you read about in the magazines and newspapers and on certain websites, and they are usually from the 22nd May to the 21st June.

Now, I say usually, because it does depend on where your Gemini was born and at what time of day.

I'll tell you why.

Here we are on Earth. Astrology is the study of the planets in their orbit around the Earth, from our viewpoint of the Earth. And even though Astrology bases its calculations on the Sun going round the Earth, which it doesn't do (the Earth goes round the Sun), it *looks* as if the Sun moves across the sky when we look up at it.

All a birth chart or natal chart is, is a little map of the sky on the day you were born. Those orbits of all the celestial bodies don't occur neatly in time with our calendars though.

So, when the magazine says Mrs Green, who was born on the 21st June, must be a Gemini, that's not entirely correct. Because if Mrs Green was born at 10pm on the 21st in New York, NY, USA, she'd actually 'be' a Cancer. She would have to be born *before* 6am on that date to be a Gemini.

People have got round this dilemma by saying things like,

"Oh, she was born on the cusp." There is no such thing as a cusp. You are either one sign of the Zodiac or another; you can't be two. The Sun will move around the sky and at a certain point it will then be in the next bit of the sky, and you're either in one bit, or the other. There is a mathematical cut-off point.

As there are 12 signs of the Zodiac, we've divided the sky into 12 bits. Each one is 30 degrees in size... this will become more apparent when we look at Bob's chart in the next chapter, but just keep that in mind.

There is no such thing as a cusp.

Try to imagine it like the dividing lines on football pitches or tennis courts. A ball is either in... or out. And anyway it's a maths thing. It's not difficult to work out now that computers do all the work.

The Twins

There is no true agreement on how the signs of the Zodiac got their names. Some historians say it's because of the shapes the stars make in the sky but if you've ever *looked* at the stars, you certainly won't see anything remotely like a twin in the sky.

More likely is the idea that the original Astrologers (the Babylonians) named the 12 signs after their gods.

Nicholas Campion tells us in his *The Dawn of Astrology* that Gemini the sign was part of the constellations and was named after Mul Mas.Tab.Bagal.Gal or as they called it 'The Great Twins'.

They first recorded the path that the Moon took along the Sun's ecliptic, its apparent path through the sky, and divided it into 18 constellations *"which stood in the path of the moon."*[2]

When the Babylonians were looking at the sky, the planets' orbits had in their backgrounds various constellations of stars. And I would just like to make a distinction here. Astrology is the study of the planets, not the stars. Stars are the twinkly things you see in the night sky and are billions of light years away from us here on Earth. Planets are celestial bodies, like the Earth, that orbit around the Sun in our 'Solar System'. Some of the planets are made of gas, some are made of rock like ours, but all of them go round and round the Sun. The Moon, our nearest neighbour, orbits around the Earth, while we orbit around the Sun.

So, Astrologers originally plotted the paths of the planets, through the sky, by matching the bits of the sky with the star constellations behind *them as you view them from Earth.*

Now, because of our orbit and a thing called the precession of the Equinoxes, those planets don't line up with the constellations anymore. So what we do now is divide the sky into 12 equal portions and start the division at the 0° Aries point at the Spring Equinox.

So now the Astrological signs match up with the seasons.

Each sign of the Zodiac has a planet that looks after it. We call it their 'ruler' and the ruler to Gemini is Mercury as there are similarities to Mercury the planet and Gemini the sign. Just to make things a bit difficult, this is also the ruler to Virgo, but that's only because there were originally 7 planets that the Babylonians used: the Sun, the Moon, Mercury, Venus, Mars, Jupiter and Saturn. It wasn't until Uranus, Neptune and Pluto were discovered that the rulerships changed, as Astrology is a living and breathing art-and-science and there is always room for change.

The Speedy Planet

Mercury is a funny little planet. It has a very erratic orbit. Sometimes it can be seen in the morning, sometimes in the evening. Goodness knows how the ancient Babylonians saw it, as it's not easy to see even with a telescope.

In our solar system it's the planet that is closest to the Sun. This makes its surface boiling hot in places, and freezing cold in others, as because of its orbit round the Sun only part of the planet actually faces the Sun. Bit like standing in front of a bonfire on a cold winter's night. If you're facing the fire, your front can get hot, but your back can get really chilly.

Mercury's orbit around the Sun is four times as fast as the Earth's, so its year is only 88 Earth days long. However, it spins so slowly on its axis that one day on Mercury is equal to 59 days on Earth. It is also the smallest planet in our solar system and is not so easy to spot; the best times being early evening in the spring and early morning in the autumn in the northern hemisphere.[3]

NASA's Messenger Probe

The American space agency NASA sent a probe called Messenger to explore the planet in 2004 and it became the first spacecraft to orbit the innermost planet on 18th March 2011. It was going to cease its investigations in March 2012, but has secured funding for an additional year of research. There is another mission planned for 2013 called BepiColombo which will carry two orbiters, one from Europe and one from Japan.[4]

So far they have discovered that the surface of Mercury is covered in volcanic explosions, craters and evidence of flood volcanism. The surface temperature is of two extremes. On the sunny side it reaches 430° C and on the dark side of the planet it goes into deep freeze with temperatures to a low -180° C. Hmm, don't fancy living there!

Mercury the Go-Between

If we look at Mercury in our solar system, we see that it stands between the Sun and us and I agree with Christina Rose who writes in her *Astrological Counselling*:

Mercury, positioned closest to the Sun, stands rather as one who introduces the solar energy to all the other planets, and vice versa. Thus, his function is that of an introductory link, transmission, connection and we may liken Mercury to a go-between, an agent or courier between the Sun and the rest of the solar system. On an incoming wavelength, this function is experienced within the individual as recognition, perception and awareness. On an out-going wavelength, it is that which spurs us toward the communication of those perceptions and awareness.[5]

Astrologers therefore think of Mercury in the birth chart as something that acts as a mediator or negotiator and helps with communication.

Mercury the Messenger God

In myth Mercury is named after the God that the Greeks called Hermes. And Hermes replaced the Babylonian god Nebo and then later the Romans named him Mercurius. This poor God had a number of name changes before it was agreed to call him Mercury.

In the Greek myths soon after being born, Hermes set off in search of the cattle belonging to his brother Apollo. He made their "hooves go backward, the front ones last and the back ones first" and hid them in the cave of the Sun god Apollo.[6]

He is also known as the trickster God because of all the naughty things he got up to.

Hermes was also the only God capable of travel to the deadly Hades underworld and back again. This is similar to the reality of the planet's surface temperatures being so extreme. Hot/cold.

Mercury is now depicted as a God with winged feet, travelling great distances with lightning speeds, being the messenger of the gods. It is these attributes that we mirror in Astrology. We're not saying that the attributes of Gemini are exactly the same as the planet Mercury, just that they're similar, that they have alike qualities.

Mercury has a dark and light side: Gemini can be bright and breezy sometimes, and dark and moody at others.

So what do other Astrologers say about Gemini?

Other Astrologers' Views

Here's Rae Orion in her *Astrology for Dummies*:

The Sunny Side

Forever young, they say. You're clever, cheerful and thoroughly interested in life. In your never-ending quest for mental stimulation, you are fascinated by the diversity of the world... when you master a skill, travel to a new place, explore a new area of knowledge, or meet someone new, you feel invigorated...

The Sorry Side

You talk too much. You drain people. You can even exhaust your own interest in an idea, simply by talking it to death. When you go into overdrive, which is often, you become nervous and tense... You're the original chameleon. [7]

Here's Christopher McIntosh in his *Astrology*:

... As Mercury is the planet of the mind, so the typical Geminian is quick-witted and resourceful. He can turn his hand to many different activities, but often finds it difficult to settle for any one. He can be something of a Jack of all trades, master of none... they also excel in written communication. Gemini is a double sign, and the Geminian often lives a double existence moving easily from one role to another.[8]

How about Linda Goodman, what's her take on Gemini?

Almost every Gemini speaks, understands or reads more than one language and French is the favourite. One way or another, the

Gemini will triumph with words. He cut his teeth on the Oxford Dictionary. He can sell ice cubes to Eskimos or dreams to a pessimist. If you happen to catch him in some dodge, he can change the subject so fast, and direct the conversation away from himself so adroitly, that the whole affair ends with you on the carpet instead of him.[9]

Let's ask Maritha Pottenger in her *Easy Astrology Guide: How to Read Your Horoscope*:

Sun in Gemini. You need to shine fluently. You may gain or seek recognition for your verbal skills. This could vary from the teacher/professor to the neighbourhood gossip, from the punster to the use of extensive vocabulary. You need to shine by being versatile. You are likely to be proud of your versatility (or ashamed of your tendency to scatter with multiple interests). Driven by wide-ranging curiosity, you may shine in diverse areas. You (also) seek recognition for your mental brilliance and for nimbleness and flexibility...[10]

Felix and Bryan tell us in *The Instant Astrologer* these Gemini keywords:

Versatile, curious, shallow, stimulating, communicative, restless, sociable, quick-witted, fickle, dexterous, ingenious, diffuse, inconsistent, chatty, artful, flippant.

Bright, sociable and communicative one day, sullen and moody the next, Gemini, the Twins, is unquestionably the most mercurial sign of the Zodiac. The fact is that, while we are all made up of many 'selves' somehow masquerading as one person, Gemini is the living embodiment of the split personality... The Twins signify Gemini's dual nature, and its challenge to get to grips with the world of opposites – for example, between light and dark, belief and cynicism, intuition and reason.[11]

I think we can safely say Gemini encompasses the attributes of communication, duality and changeability.

Loving to Communicate and Languages

This is the quality that a Gemini excels at. Being heard and understood. If you want to understand something, get a Gemini to explain it. They love to explain things. It's not that they want to appear more clever than you; they just enjoy the process of passing on information.

Ulrika lives and works in Zurich, Switzerland as a translator and teacher. She tells us a bit about her Gemini self:

What I think is typical Gemini in me is that I am very fast, on the road, in picking things up, trends... I 'find' things long before they become a trend, or mainstream. I am definitely a messenger and conveyor of information to others.

I asked her how many languages does she speak? *"Five"* was her answer.

I then asked Veronica about her language ability. She lives in the UK in a large metropolitan university city and works there as a lecturer:

Well, I'm a bit rusty with some of them, but I know/have known at least a bit of these languages in varying degrees: Ancient Greek, Modern Greek, Latin, French, Norwegian, Swedish, Danish, Spanish, Welsh; and if I weren't so lazy these days I would have been learning a bit of Portuguese and Serbo-Croat, because it doesn't feel right to me to go on holiday abroad and not know anything of the language.

One language I like but have never managed to learn is Icelandic, because classes conflicted with my working hours when I was studying Scandinavian languages. I am fluent in Norwegian, almost bilingual, as well as my mother tongue English & can translate from Swedish and Danish better than my oral skills might suggest.

I then asked her what her favourite form of communication is. Is it e-mail, letter, phone or face-to-face?

You forgot telepathy!

E-mail is the easiest (I used to love letter-writing before we had e-mail, and found it a real lifeline e.g. during my marriage), but erotic texting is great fun. Phone can be great, especially with people who are not so good at being present when you are with them in physical reality – they pretty much have to make an effort on the phone!

I also love receiving handwritten letters and really enjoy good handwriting; in fact it can even be a turn on. (I am also interested in graphology.) In affairs of the heart I think to write the object of desire a letter – or poem – would be most appropriate.

Face-to-face communication works best with some people, but it depends on the individual. I go for whatever will be the most satisfying mode of communication with the individual in question.

Among other hobbies she even liked learning Greek at school!

Ancient Greek, Modern Greek (which I was teaching myself for fun), Latin, French, English, swimming, riding, reading, specially poetry, creative writing...

Julie is a British citizen but now lives and works in Florence in Italy. She tells us her preferences:

Communication – I prefer face-to-face to talk and chat, then the telephone. I use my mobile to send messages and arrange where to meet friends etc. I'm a bit lazy to send e-mail and letters, quicker to pick up the phone and talk.

Kotryna is a student of creative writing in Lithuania. I asked her about her communication style:

It depends... Sometimes I have periods when I want to hide from the whole world and just pretend I don't exist; then a face-to-face case is out of question. Of course, virtual communication is barely acceptable then, too, but it's a compromise. I like to multitask a lot of things, so typing (Skype, Facebook chat) is best then, because I can do many things at a time (and talk to many people at a time!). But sometimes I really crave real human contact. When I ask to see someone live, it usually means I want some time with them alone, without distractions, and I hate it when that person comes not alone without a warning. I am not a big fan of letters because they're not fast enough for me. Even e-mails. I love a live flowing conversation. Letters are good when you want to say something without being interrupted and need to really think about phrasing carefully.

Mandana lives and works in Indonesia and has a number of Gemini friends. I asked her what was their favourite form of communication and how many phones (mobile or otherwise) did they have.

What form of communication do they like the most? Face-to-face, phone, text, computer/e-mail or letter?

The faster the better, and the more direct the better. So their most favourite in descending order would be face-to-face, telephoning, texting, and posting on social networks. E-mailing and writing letters are just NOT FAST ENOUGH.

How many mobile phones/telephones do they have? Please include all mobiles they don't use, and the landline phones in their house.

On average, two cell phone numbers (1 GSM and 1 CDMA), one of them probably a BlackBerry. Plus one not-too-frequently used landline belonging to the house.

Veronica has a story to tell about her phone use:

I have a landline with three handsets and an answer machine. Two mobiles in current use, one mainly as a spare camera. Nothing flash. (One was manna from heaven – found in bits on a country road, but better than mine, and weirdly the same model as my grand-daughter's. It meant she could Skype me whenever she needed while she was going through a really difficult time in her life.) Most of my mobiles have been hand-me-downs. And I still have all my old mobiles from about 2000 onwards (about four) that don't work, but I keep meaning to get them wiped so I can give them to charity. It's just never urgent enough to do today!

Languages of every sort are loved by Geminis. My ex used to tell me his grandmother spoke "English, Yiddish and Rubbish", and even though he'd tell you he wasn't bilingual, he certainly knew enough Yiddish to understand and chat with members of his family.

Ulrika (who we met earlier) speaks five languages:

I am the founder and editor of a bilingual home exchange website. Main activities include customer service in several languages and writing about the subject to promote the idea. Home exchanging is an amazing way to travel. You get to meet the locals and you are treated like a guest. You are never a tourist. Many times your hosts become your friends. We have stayed in an Italian palazzo, a medieval tower, a 250 year old English cottage, an elegant American contemporary home and on and on – all for free.

Duality

Wherever I am I always find myself looking out the window wishing I was somewhere else.
Angelina Jolie

I know so many Geminis and I've seen their multiple takes on life. Sometimes you never know who you are going to meet next time you see them, and they're perfectly happy about this ability to be changeable in mood and thought.

As John Wayne, a Gemini Sun with Moon in Scorpio, said:

Each of us is a mixture of some good and some not so good qualities. In considering one's fellow man it's important to remember the good things...We should refrain from making judgments just because a fella happens to be a dirty, rotten SOB.

Which is such a typical Gemini statement it made me laugh!

Joan Collins the English actress has married five times. Marilyn Monroe married and divorced three times. Nicole Kidman the actress has married twice. Prince the singer has been engaged once and married twice. Judy Garland another actress married five times. Bob Dylan has been married and divorced twice. Tom Jones married once but had numerous affairs. Brooke Shields has been married twice. Bob Hope married twice and also had numerous affairs. Ray Davies married three times so did Paul McCartney, and John Wayne married three times and divorced twice.

However, don't get the idea that *all* Geminis marry more than once. There are plenty that marry and are perfectly happy, my aunt being one of them.

The point I am making is, if a Gemini has lost interest in something, or taken their eye off the ball, they will want 'change'. And mostly that change will centre around something they can 'do', rather than change within themselves. Bob Dylan and Prince both changed their religious views and converted to other religions.

If you want a little glimpse into Gemini changeability, then look at some of the art by Damien Hirst.

Violet is a mum and writer, and lives and works in Wales. I asked her what was one of her Gemini traits:

> *Two families in different countries... liking to have two or more of some things (but never sets, e.g. of china).*

Sexual Duality

> *I've fancied other women, but I haven't done anything about it.*
> Kylie Minogue

Isadora Duncan, the dancer, is a classic example of sexual duality. Not only did she have a number of relationships before marrying, she then had an affair and also a relationship with another woman; so if nothing else, her sexuality was certainly changeable.

Angelina Jolie has no qualms about admitting she had feelings both ways:

> *They're right to think that about me, because I'm the person most likely to sleep with my female fans; I genuinely love other women. And I think they know that.*

Actor Ian McKellen didn't 'come out' until he was in his 40s. He said that actors of his generation:

> *spent so long pretending to be straight, to be someone else, that eventually we became very good at it. There was no Graham Norton on the television at that time, no gay MPs, no one talking about gay*

rights on the radio. So I dealt with it by trying to cut that part of myself off, to hide myself, to choke a part of me.

In a talk he gave to school pupils in London he said he:

wished that every child, every teacher, every person in this room can be free to be who they are, whatever their sexual orientation.

Another more famous example of sexual experimentation and duality is the Marquis de Sade, an 18th Century French aristocrat who not only indulged in extreme activities but also became famous in later life for his writings. One was titled *The 120 Days of Sodom, or the School of Licentiousness* which he wrote while imprisoned in the Bastille for poisoning and sodomy. He had a Scorpio Ascendant which I expect contributed towards this lifestyle...

Just as their sign depicts the Twins, there are numerous options and alternatives to the sexuality of a Gemini. Nothing is permanent or enduring.

Changeability

Diana is in her 30s and lives and works in New York City. She succinctly sums up her Gemini-ness:

Had over 30 jobs lifetime & moved 15 times or a few more. Fave subject: English. Hobbies: reading, talking, more like sermonizing, lol. Also researching spiritual and occult matters, exercising, walking. Two languages.

Rosemary is 31 and lives in Northampton, UK and works in retail management. I asked her about change.

How many times have you moved home/job in your life so far?

Since the age of 18 I have moved home approx 18 times. Since the age of 14 I have had approx 17 jobs.

What were your favourite subjects at school, what are your hobbies now?

I enjoyed art at school. My hobbies now are travelling, crafts, although I'm unsure of what at the moment. I designed jewellery for a while, but got bored with that. I'm thinking of Fashion and maybe a little acting course on the side. I've very recently discovered my spiritual side, so I want to discover that more.

Rebecca is in her early 50s and lives and works as a college tutor in Portsmouth, England. She also has had a lot of change in her life:

Loads. Had about 20 jobs and only about 20 homes and I'm 51, so not so Gemini perhaps.

I thought it was funny when she said *"not so Gemini"*. I know people who have lived in the same house and had the same job their whole lives...

What were your favourite subjects at school, what are your hobbies now?

Languages and sport at school. Sport, walking in mountains, coffee or wine with friends, astrology.

As before, Mandana tells us about her Gemini friends/relatives in Indonesia:

How many jobs/side jobs/businesses do they have, whether full-time or part-time?

Generally they have one full-time job, one part-time job helping a friend, and one small business selling something. My cousin works as a producer at a TV station and sells cookies and muffins on the side; my brother works as a marketer at a TV station and helps his friend deal with the friend's clothes shop; my mother sells Hajj packages for people wanting to go on the Hajj pilgrimage to Mecca and also sells women's clothes, head scarves, bags, shawls and accessories to friends and family as she find the time and money to shop.

What is the nature of their work?

Marketing, directing people, selling – including selling services.

Gemini Clint Eastwood has some strong views about change:

I do agree that when you get to a certain stage in life, you change. And you should change. People ask if you've changed since such and such. Well, of course I've changed. Now whether I've changed for the better or for the worse becomes another point. If a person is constantly evolving, constantly reading new material and being exposed to new material and growing in life, then you're becoming, hopefully, a more intelligent and well-rounded individual. If you're not then something's wrong and you're sliding back in the other direction.

He obviously has change wired into his psyche, but it's not always so correct to say that change is necessarily a sign of development. The fixed signs: Taurus, Leo and Scorpio are very reluctant to change, and find it in some cases distressing.

English actor and Gemini Hugh Laurie has another view on change. For him no matter what he's doing, it's as if the grass is always greener on the other side:

I think I'm the kind of person who'd always want to be doing the thing I'm not currently doing. I've got this perennially mournful, wistful aching to be doing something else.[12]

Gemini Actress Helena Bonham Carter likes to change the way she looks:

I love changing what I look like because I always feel super strange whenever I do watch something that I'm in.

This Gemini love of change can be marriage, as we saw with Joan Collins and others, or it can be work or house location.

I asked Rebecca how many times she has moved home/job in her life so far:

Homes: only 16 places in 67 years. Jobs – very few. Was bringing up children for several years. Only about 4 jobs really, one for 22 years. But I was doing bits of other, mostly pro bono, work at times, and much more these days.

Ulrika lives and works in Switzerland as a translator.

I've moved home 11 times and changed job 10 times.

If you have a Gemini working for you, then don't expect them to work with you forever. If there is one thing that Geminis change a lot, it's their job/s. They especially love jobs that take them places, or where they can flit between two locations. I had a boss who loved the fact that his job wasn't just office-based. He could go out and meet clients/buyers/suppliers and his day could be as varied as he wanted. Travelling salesmen/women always come to mind with Geminis.

As we are going to work with the chart of Bob Dylan, here are the changes that happened in his life.

He changed his name from Robert Allen Zimmerman to Bob

Dylan in 1962. He was born to Jewish parents and converted to Christianity in the late 1970s.

He's written the songs:

Times Have Changed, I Feel a Change Comin' On, Gonna Change My Way of Thinking (if that isn't a Gemini titled song I don't know what is!!), *Things Have Changed* and the album *The Times They are a-Changing*.

He changed from being a folk singer and playing acoustic guitar to electric, which caused a lot of controversy at the time. In 1986 he experimented with a bit of rap music and by the 2000s he'd covered rockabilly, Western swing, jazz, and lounge ballads.

You cannot accuse him of standing still for long! He has also been married and divorced twice.

Chapter Two

How to Make a Chart

Making a chart is so much easier now. When my lovely auntie was into Astrology, she had to draw up charts using complicated formulae, mathematical bits with longitude and latitude, taking into account time of day then all that stuff about 'Daylight Saving'... I'm very glad that computers were invented and computer software to calculate it all.

All we need to know today are three pieces of information:

The date the person was born.
The place they were born.
And **the time** they were born.

That's it!

Oh dear, I hear you say, I don't know what time my Gemini was born! This is when you have to become a bit of a detective, as without the time of birth, your chart won't be accurate.

In some countries, Scotland and parts of the USA, the time of birth is written on the birth certificate.

If your Gemini was born as a twin in the UK (Yes! It does happen!) the time will be recorded on the birth certificate, because everyone needs to know who is the older baby.

If you don't have that sort of record, you will need to ask the mother or father, who if you're lucky might remember; though if your Gemini was born more than 30 years ago, accuracy and memory might be a little lacking. Sometimes families write birth times in the family Bible (ours did), or sometimes there's a birthday book, and again it might be noted there. Or if you're really lucky, you will have a relative who is into Astrology and they will have faithfully recorded your birth data. I'm one of those as my lovely auntie recorded my birth data in her Ephemeris. Thank you, Auntie Jo!!

If you don't have the time, don't worry. You can still find out what sign your Gemini's planets are in, not their location, so you will have to skip Chapters Three and Five.

First of all we need to find a good website that's free and accurate. The website we're going to use is based in Switzerland in a place called Zollikon, overlooking Lake Zurich. I went to school in Zurich so I know how lovely that view is! Astrodienst which means 'Astro Service' is a website real, live Astrologers use. It has over 6 million visitors per month and over 16,000 members, so you will be in good company.

Go to http://www.astro.com and make an account.

They will ask for your e-mail and nothing else (unless you want to add it).

You can create a chart as a 'guest user' or do what I recommend, which is to create a 'free registered user profile'. This means every time you log in, the site will know it's you and it makes life much easier.

After you have entered all your data –

Date
Time
Location of birth

– we can now get your chart made.

Go to the page marked 'free horoscopes' and scroll down the page until you see the section marked:

Extended Chart Selection

Click on this link and you'll be taken to a page that's got lots of boxes but the main headings on the left are:

Birth Data
Methods
Options
Image size
Additional objects

Add all your info into the boxes if you haven't already, then click on the section marked House System under the heading Options.

Scroll down until you see 'equal' and click on that. This makes your chart into equal segments, and is the system this book is based on.

Now click the blue button 'Click here to show chart' and 'bing'!! Your chart will appear in another window.

Equal House System vs. Placidus System

The default system on this website, and most websites and computer programmes, except the ones I use, are set to a system called Placidus. This makes each house, which we will learn about in Chapter Five, unequal sizes... and to my mind looks scraggy and uneven.

The Equal House system is the oldest system and the one the ancients used before Mr Placidus came along and made some changes.

According to Herbert T. Waite in *The New Waite's Compendium of Natal Astrology* in 1917, the Placidus System is:

... most widely used at the present day, seventeenth century, generally adopted in England in the eighteenth century, and now (quite mistakenly) supposed, by those no better informed, to be the standard traditional system, simply because tables of houses based on it...were published a century ago, and have since been imitated and continued, and enable students to copy the houses from them without any inquiry as to what they mean. The ordinary tables of

houses on sale are really tables of the 'Houses According to Placidus'.[13]

Most people don't use the hard copy books of tables, we use computer programmes; but still over 100 years since Herbert wrote the above, that 'system' is just randomly copied on and on without much consideration given to what the system is, or how it works. Suffice to know that there are about six main 'systems' and Equal House is the oldest. More about this in Chapter Five.

In the centre of the chart, the segments (which are called houses) are numbered 1–12 in an anticlockwise order.

These are the shapes representing the signs, so find the one that matches yours. They are called glyphs.

Aries ♈
Taurus ♉
Gemini ♊
Cancer ♋
Leo ♌
Virgo ♍
Libra ♎
Scorpio ♏
Sagittarius ♐
Capricorn ♑
Aquarius ♒
Pisces ♓

The Elements

To understand your Gemini fully, you must take into account which Element their Ascendant and Moon are in.

Each sign of the Zodiac has been given an element that it operates under: Earth, Air, Fire and Water. I like to think of them as operating at different 'speeds'.

The **Earth** signs are **Taurus, Virgo** and **Capricorn**. The Earth Element is stable, grounded and concerned with practical matters. A Gemini with a lot of Earth in their chart works best at a very slow, steady speed. (I refer to these in the text as 'Earthy'.)

The **Air** signs are our friend **Gemini, Libra** and **Aquarius** (who is the 'Water-carrier' *not* a Water sign). The Air element enjoys ideas, concepts and thoughts. It operates at a faster speed than Earth, not as fast as Fire but faster than Water and Earth. Imagine them as being medium speed. (I might call them Airy or Air sign in the text.)

The **Fire** signs are **Aries, Leo** and **Sagittarius**. The Fire element likes action, excitement and can be very impatient. Their speed is *very* fast. (I refer to these as Firey i.e. Fire-Sign.)

The **Water** signs are **Cancer, Scorpio** and **Pisces**. The Water element involves feelings, impressions, hunches and intuition. They operate faster than Earth but not as fast as Air. A sort of slow-medium speed. (I refer to these as Watery as in Water sign.)

Chapter Three

The Ascendant

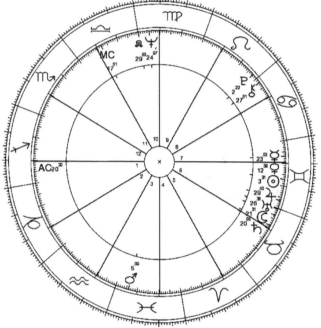

Name: ♂ Bob Dylan
born on Sa., 24 May 1941
in Duluth, MN (US)
92w06, 46n47

Time: 9:05 p.m.
Univ.Time: 3:05 25 May
Sid. Time: 13:05:51

ASTRO DIENST
www.astro.com
Type: 2.GW 0.0-1 5-Okt-2012

Natal Chart (Method: Web Style / equal)
Sun sign: Gemini
Ascendant: Sagittarius

Now you will have made your chart, or until you're feeling confident you can use the one I've made above.

This is Bob Dylan's chart. You can make it too. His data is at the back of this book but I'll add it here so you can follow me.

Date: 24th May 1941
Place: Duluth, MN, USA
Time: 9.05pm

I spent quite a time trying to decide whose chart to use for this book, as it had to be someone *most* people had heard of. It was a toss-up between Paul McCartney or Bob Dylan and I plumped with Bob because Paul is famous for being part of the Beatles, while Bob is famous in his own right. Anyway, that was my thinking.

The chart you will make will have lots of lines going across it from planet to planet.

Ignore them.

I've made Bob's chart without those 'aspects' lines just to make it easier to pinpoint the things we need to know.

At the moment, it will all look like gobbledygook. Don't worry, it's not that difficult.

If you look at the quarter to nine position on the horizontal line going across the chart from right to left, you'll see the initials AC and in very small writing the numbers 20.

This is Astro-speak for: "Bob's Ascendant is 20 degrees and 20 minutes in the sign of Sagittarius."

Mary, how the heck did we get Sagittarius?

Look again.

That AC initial is right slap bang in the middle of the symbol for Sagittarius, which looks like an arrow.

What are you talking about, Mary, I thought you said Bob is a Gemini?

Yes, he certainly is a Gemini but because he was born at 9.05pm the sign that was rising on the eastern horizon was Sagittarius... and we call that bit of the sky the Ascendant or rising sign.

It's not a planet.

It's not the Sun or Moon; they are different parts of the chart.

The Ascendant is where the chart starts. It's defined by the moment the person became alive, took their first breath, started living on Earth as opposed to being in Mum's tummy.

The Moment of Birth

Astrologers consider the Ascendant an auspicious moment in time.

Isn't it?

Isn't the minute you arrive in your world *the* most important point in time in your life?

Well, that's how Astrologers consider it.

Because the Ascendant is determined by the time of birth, if Bob had been born at 9.05am (in the morning), his Ascendant sign would be in the sign of Leo. So you can now understand why getting the right *time* of birth is important. If your time is wrong not only will your Ascendant be wrong but also all the other bits in the chart will be in different places.

The importance Astrology gives to the Ascendant is to help us learn how someone tackles their life. It's sort of like their Life's Path. If the Ascendant is in the sign of Capricorn, then the 'view' of the life path is in a more down-to-earth and practical way than if it were in the sign of Pisces, where they'd be more in touch with feelings and fairies.

The Ascendant is thought to also represent how you react in an acutely stressful situation, how you begin a project... someone with a Fire sign Ascendant will approach a project in a much swifter way than someone with an Earth sign Ascendant. Think of it as your First Aid sign and remember the speeds I described in the last chapter.

Bob's Ascendant is in Sagittarius: a swift Fire sign, so he can make snap judgements, he's happy with international relations and enjoys other cultures and ways of life. Different spiritualities have been explored with Judaism and Christianity, and he is sometimes referred to as a preacher, as well as a singer. He is also content to 'say-it-as-it-is' and doesn't mind offending if he thinks he's right.

But underneath this exterior, there are still the Gemini flights of fancy, the Gemini needing to communicate, ask questions, add variety, and constantly searching and questioning.

So here are the various Ascendants, in Zodiac order, that your Gemini could have. Look at your chart and find the one that corresponds to your Gemini and have a read. It will help you understand them a little better.

Aries Ascendant

You were once wild here. Don't let them tame you.
Isadora Duncan

Ruled by brave Mars the God of War, the Aries Ascendant will give the person the attitude to come out of their corner fighting. They're heroic, bold and daring, and can generally be accused of going bravely where Angels fear to tread. For a Gemini, this Ascendant makes them more self-assured and slightly more impatient.

Taurus Ascendant

Now I need to take a piece of wood and make it sound like the railroad track, but I also had to make it beautiful and lovable so that a person playing it would think of it in terms of his mistress, a bartender, his wife, a good psychiatrist – whatever.
Les Paul

Taurus Ascendant wants to slow down and smell the roses as they wend their way through life. Don't hurry them, don't nag; this is a slower, more determined Ascendant that wants to be sure, safe and satisfied. A Gemini might struggle to align this part of their psyche and might resist the ponderous energy of it... and rush off on a new project, then find later down the line that they feel unsure, or anxious. Slow and Steady should be their motto.

Gemini Ascendant

The important thing is not what they think of me, but what I think of them.
Queen Victoria

Now we get to doubling up. To be a Gemini (the Twins) and have Gemini Ascendant means there are four people in the room all needing satisfaction. Help! How to satisfy all those people! Variety, movement, change are all on the menu, and it will help to satisfy the eternal 'grass-is-always-greener-on-the-other-side' outlook. They came into the world asking questions. Their biggest question is, "Why me?"

Cancer Ascendant

I'm just glad I was able to return to some of that innocence and beauty I had as a child when I started my own family, and my children brought me back some of that spirit.
Angelina Jolie

The view with Cancer Ascendant will always firmly be on their family and things close to home. It makes a Gemini more interested in that which is traditional, home-based and family-orientated. They love nothing more than sharing their wisecracks and humour with those that are 'of the same blood', be that literal or figurative.

Leo Ascendant

Everyone has inside of him a piece of good news. The good news is that you don't know how great you can be! How much you can love! What you can accomplish!
Anne Frank

Look at me!! This should really be the Leo Ascendant catch-phrase. They love attention of any sort. They are sunny, upbeat, mostly happy and mostly optimistic. They love attention and dramatic displays of affection… "Darling!!" The worst thing you can do is ignore them, as they will then fade away into grumpiness.

Virgo Ascendant

The more constraints one imposes, the more one frees one's self. And the arbitrariness of the constraint serves only to obtain precision of execution.
Igor Stravinsky

This is the sign that enjoys being able to absorb the detail of something. They like to take their time knowing *exactly* how something works; being vague doesn't happen. They can happily spend hours collecting data, or categorising things either mentally or literally. They might not be tidy, but their minds are active with thinking about being tidy.

Libra Ascendant

Everyone has a right to be in love and consummate that love.
Paula Abdul

Relationships and significant others rate highly with Libra. Their heart needs to be encased in warm fuzziness, and for no one to argue or fall out. Ruled by Venus the Goddess of Love, they want love with a capital 'L', and romance and flowers are high on the agenda. If they are not in a relationship, I would prescribe one as they're only truly happy being able to share with someone, equally and fairly.

Scorpio Ascendant

I would describe myself as emotional and highly strung. If something upsets me, it really upsets me. If something makes me angry, I get really angry. But it's all very upfront. I can't hide it. I'm also loyal and I hope I'm fun.
Nicole Kidman

Intensity is their watchword. Trust is also an important issue. Every task is approached with vigour and concentration. This is not a fluffy sign. Ruled by Pluto the planet of deep transformation, this gives a Gemini the ability to go boldly where others might not even think about. Their emotions are strong and their memories long.

Sagittarius Ascendant

People seldom do what they believe in. They do what is convenient, then repent.
Bob Dylan

Aiming their arrows of discovery high into the sky, Sagittarius Ascendant for a Gemini brings a searching, curious attitude that never seems to be satisfied. They love international relations, exploring other cultures and their beliefs, and if they think they're right, no amount of discussion or argument will make them change their mind. However, being a Gemini, they can change, but only when they are ready.

Capricorn Ascendant

I work very hard and I'm worth every cent.
Naomi Campbell

Ruled by severe Saturn the God of restraint and fiscal responsibility, their life view revolves around that for which they must work hard. They are ambitious and forward focused and their fear is lack of resources and/or money. Consequently when they've worked out where they are going, nothing will stand in their way and like a climber not a comet, they will reach that apex.

Aquarius Ascendant

You can probably get something more from a wall than a person sometimes.
Ray Davies

A more zany and weird Ascendant to have for a Gemini and ruled by Uranus the Wacky Planet, this can bring someone who wants to 'be different'. They also yearn for freedom and hate instruction, orders, rules and regulations, and anything that holds them back from exploring. More focused on groups rather than individuals, and definitely altruistic.

Pisces Ascendant

If slaughterhouses had glass walls, everyone would be a vegetarian.
Paul McCartney

Fairies, soft Angel singing, connecting with the cosmos and the expanses of creation appeal to this Ascendant. Fuzzy thinking and tardiness can be the result. They love the esoteric and that which can't be explained. They can sense someone's hurt from 50 paces and will do anything to prevent further suffering. Ruled by Neptune the Water god, splashing about with emotions and feelings reigns.

Chapter Four

The Moon

If the Sun in Astrology represents 'who' we are and our 'ego', then the Moon, as in real life which reflects the light of the Sun, represents how we feel about things, as opposed to what we think.

This is fine if your Sun sign and Moon sign match up, but it gets more tricky if your Moon sign doesn't complement the energies of your Sun sign.

Imagine you're a Gemini, which is a fast-thinking Air sign, who has Moon in Capricorn, which is a slow-moving Earth sign that likes to do things the 'proper' way.

Imagine also that you want to buy a house, and the Gemini part of you wants to go ahead, and get it all done in minutes flat but your emotional self (your Moon) is feeling:

This is too fast, we need to think about this for a while and check we've got all the facts, and the history of the house and... we also need to know about the neighbours because without good neighbours life can be miserable...

So one part of you is pushing for a result, and the other part is holding back and feeling unsure and a teeny bit frightened about making such a big step.

This is when Sun sign Astrology falls apart. Without knowing the true extent of the possibilities in your chart, you might gaily go through life never understanding why you do one thing and something else happens. I like to think that I keep ALL the parts of my chart happy, and as a Pisces with Moon in Gemini I have an inkling of understanding of opposing astrological forces. I need to have variety and change but I also need to be 'at-one' with the cosmos and all things mystical.

I find in private practice, when someone comes for a reading or a consultation, that the bit of the chart that mostly 'needs help' is the Moon. As, generally speaking, our rational self overpowers our emotional self... and when our poor little Moons need a bit of TLC, you'll be pleased to know, we have a suitable solution.

This is the symbol for the Moon. ☽ In our example chart, Bob has his Moon in the sign of Taurus, making him enjoy life's 'simple' pleasures.

The Dr Bach Flower Essences

In 1933 Dr Edward Bach, a medical doctor and Homeopath, published a little booklet called *The Twelve Healers and Other Remedies*. His theory was that if the emotional component a person was suffering from was removed, their 'illness' would also disappear. I tend to agree with this kind of thinking as most illnesses (except being hit by a bus) are preceded by an unhappy event or an emotional disruption that then sets into place the body getting out of sync. Removing the emotional issue and bringing a bit of stability into someone's life, when they are having a hard time, can improve their overall health so much that wellness resumes.

Knowing which Bach Flower Essence can help certain worries and upsetments gives you and your Gemini more control over your lives. I recommend the essences a lot in my practice if I feel a certain part of a person's chart is under stress... and usually it's the Moon that needs help. The essences describe the negative aspects of the character, which are focused on during treatment. This awareness helps reverse those trends, so when our emotional selves are nice and comfortable, we can then face each day with more strength.

I've quoted Dr Bach's actual words for each sign.

To use the essences take two drops from the stock bottle and put them into a glass of water and sip. I tend to recommend putting them into a small water bottle, and sipping them throughout the day, at least four times. For young children, do the same.

Remember to seek medical attention if symptoms don't get better and/or seek professional counselling.

Aries Moon

I happen to be one of the people who forced safety down the throats of track owners and car manufacturers.
Jackie Stewart

This is the Moon of action and energy. As Aries is so exuberant and assertive they are basically sitting on an emotional volcano. Feelings are swift, fast and energetic, and are expressed powerfully and impetuously. If they become cross, like a storm it all blows over eventually and they hold no grudges. The most obvious benefit of this is the honesty of their gut reaction to events.

Bach Flower Essence Impatiens:

Those who are quick in thought and action and who wish all things to be done without hesitation or delay.

Taurus Moon

I mean, even my dressing room at the studio has candles and cushions and cashmere rugs and things.
Joan Collins

As a fixed sign Taurus Moon makes for an emotionally consistent person, slow to change their heart. This is fine, but they must be aware of hanging on to outdated feelings. Additionally when their earthy, sensual side meets the Moon's natural appreciation of luxury, it can make them one of the Zodiac's self-indulgent lovers of good living. Due to this tendency to emotional and material fascination, they find it more difficult to be poor or let go of possessions.

Bach Flower Essence Gentian:

Those who are easily discouraged. They may be progressing well in the affairs of their daily life, but any small delay or hindrance to progress causes doubt and soon disheartens them.

Gemini Moon

I love listening to new stuff; at home in LA I always have the radio on to hear what is happening.
Tom Jones

Gemini's airy, abstract energy when experienced as the Moon makes them more likely to analyse and rationalise their feelings. The plus side of this is the clarity of their self-knowledge; the minus is things just go round and round in their head until the only solution is to turn off their brain for a while. Talking about their feelings helps; feeling their feelings is more difficult so writing them down or putting them into poetry helps.

Bach Flower Essence Cerato:

Those who have not sufficient confidence in themselves to make their own decisions.

Cancer Moon

When we recall the past, we usually find that it is the simplest things – not the great occasions – that in retrospect give off the greatest glow of happiness.
Bob Hope

This makes for a double portion of lunar influence, as the Moon in Cancer is in its own zodiacal home. Astrology regards this as a highly 'maternal' influence, and that the emotions will be well tuned in to protecting and nurturing others. It can make for more tears and more emotion than other Moons, and I always recommend keeping a Moon Diary to check the emotional temperature.

Bach Flower Essence Clematis:

Living in the hopes of happier times, when their ideals may come true.

Leo Moon

JK Rowling said Bellatrix's role was going to be significant in the last one, when I showed some reluctance in playing a tiny bit part.
Helena Bonham Carter

Leo's traditional love of being in the limelight means that Moon-in-Leo people are likely to have an instinct for being the centre of attention. Red carpets, adoring fans, friends and family are all appreciated. You can't use too many superlatives, or thank them too much. They love to bathe in the warm glow of appreciation for just being who they are, and emotional respect is a must.

Bach Flower Essence Vervain:

Those with fixed principles and ideas, which they are confident are right.

Virgo Moon

My ambition is to get better as an actor. I still think there's room for improvement.
Ian McKellen

This is a slightly trickier Moon for a Gemini as Virgo Moons are often seen as somewhat problematic due to the Virgoan emphasis on order and harmony, which can sit uncomfortably with our notoriously uncontrollable emotions. And because Virgo is a mutable, changeable sign it means that the emotions will be fluid and hard to define. Needing perfection will drive them to distraction, and wanting *everything* to be perfect a continual goal.

Bach Flower Essence Centaury:

Their good nature leads them to do more than their own share of work and they may neglect their own mission in life.

Libra Moon

Ours is a nonviolent movement that depends on faith in the human predilection for fair play and compassion.
Aung San Suu Kyi

Libran energy puts a strong emphasis on harmony and balance. This is fine for the individual alone, and is often seen as giving the Moon-in-Libra person a refined aesthetic awareness, naturally good instincts or 'taste'. Slightly trickier is the question of relations with others. The fear of expressing emotions which will cause difficult scenes mean that Moon-Librans may say one thing while secretly feeling and doing another, and that can lead to accusations of indecisiveness.

Bach Flower Essence Scleranthus:

Those who suffer from being unable to decide between two things, first one seeming right then the other.

Scorpio Moon

You have so much to share, you have so much to tell, you have so

much you want to expose, so much that's inside that you've learned from that life period. There are really very few people I can share that with.
Priscilla Presley

Scorpio's notorious association with murky depths means this is where their emotions will be found, and that can make them hard to get to grips with. The word 'deep' recurs in astrological descriptions of this combination: deep longings, deep passions. If you think of the colour of deep red blood, you'll get more of an idea of how this Moon feels. Nothing is superficial; everything is profound.

Bach Flower Essence Chicory:

They are continually correcting what they consider wrong and enjoy doing so.

Sagittarius Moon

I'm studying the Kabbalah, which is really the essence of Jewish Spirituality.
Sandra Bernhard

Sagittarius Moon loves to explore the deeper expanses of the mind. It isn't sufficient for them to just know 'stuff'; they want to know the *deeper meaning* behind the stuff. When they're stressed, they are looking for spiritual solutions. The bigger 'Why' with the bigger answer 'Because'. They also enjoy reading spiritual texts, or at the very least travelling to other countries and supping cool cocktails on exotic beaches.

This Essence comes under the heading 'Over-Sensitive to Influences and Ideas'.

Bach Flower Essence Agrimony:

They hide their cares behind their humour and jesting and try to bear their trials with cheerfulness.

Capricorn Moon

I was angry and frustrated until I started my own family and my first child was born. Until then I didn't really appreciate life the way I should have, but fortunately I woke up.
Johnny Depp

Of the Moon signs Capricorn is probably the most challenging. It is ruled by scary Saturn, the grim reaper and planet of hard knocks, so their emotional make-up is severe and self-flagellating. Like Scorpio Moon, they can absorb more negativity than other signs but it makes them fearful of more pain. 'Stop beating yourself up' would be a good motto. Capricorn loves the tough material reality of the world, while the Moon is the 'inner child', and may not feel at all at home in this strict environment. They may patronise their emotions as foolish or trivial, and this can lead to over-seriousness, but this is only a replacement for the real need – the security of 'real emotion', not just 'feelings'.

Bach Flower Essence Mimulus:

Fear of worldly things, illness, pain, accident, poverty, of dark, of being alone, of misfortune. They secretly bear their dread and do not speak freely of it to others.

Aquarius Moon

I am involved in a freedom ride protesting the loss of the remaining minority rights of the few earthbound stars.
Marilyn Monroe

I have come across a number of people with Aquarius Moons.

That Aquarius flavour can make them so detached from their emotions that they find it hard to express their feelings. They may find their emotions hard to get to grips with as Aquarian energy is airy and gives them a natural tendency to consider them in an abstract way. Equally, it is a fixed energy, and emotions are famously fluid and hard to pin down. The result is they are very unlikely to wear their heart on their sleeve and may seem emotionally cool.

Bach Flower Essence Water Violet:

For those who like to be alone, very independent, capable and self-reliant. They are aloof and go their own way.

Pisces Moon

The only thing that can save the world is the reclaiming of the awareness of the world. That's what poetry does.
Allen Ginsberg

If you're involved with a Gemini with a Pisces Moon, take a deep breath. This makes for an especially sensitive soul, and if your Gemini is a boy *please* treat him gently. He'll certainly be creative, musical, inspired, talented *but* he might not know what day of the week it is, where he put his watch, wallet, money or bus fare. Pisces is the most intrinsically emotional of the signs and can have access to acute emotional sensitivity, which makes life complicated, and action difficult.

This Essence comes under the heading 'For Those Who Have Fear' and will help this fragile, gentle soul take courage to face any emergency be it death of a beloved pet to starting school.

Bach Flower Essence Rock Rose:

For cases where there even appears no hope or when the person is very frightened or terrified.

Chapter Five

The Houses

So now we've learned about the Sun and the Moon; let's find out a little more about the birth chart we have created on www.astro.com.

If you look carefully at the chart we've made, you'll see the numbers 1–12 going anticlockwise (counterclockwise) around the inside of the circle. The segments of the chart, which make it look a bit like a pizza, are called 'houses'. They used to be called 'mansions' by ancient Astrologers as they 'house' the location of a planet.

Remember, your birth chart is like a little map of the sky taken on the day you were born and has to 'house' all the planets, not just the Sun and Moon. We won't go into the interpretation of all the other planets; we're just going to look at our map and find the location of the Sun.

Now, we know, obviously, that the Sun was in the *sign* of Gemini on the day your relative/friend/lover was born but what we're going to find out now is in which particular *part* of the chart is their symbol for the Sun . ☉

If they were born early in the morning, just as the Sun was rising, their Sun symbol would be somewhere near the Ascendant or the beginning of the chart. If they were born round-about lunchtime, then the Sun would have been high in the sky in houses 9 or 10, above the horizon in the upper part of the chart.

If you imagine that the centre of the chart is the Earth spinning in space, if that person was born during daylight, their Sun symbol would be above the Earth (literally)... equally if they were born when it was dark, their Sun symbol would be below the Earth in the 'houses' marked from about 2–6.

In our example chart Bob was born at 9.05pm in the evening,

so if you look at his chart you will see that his Sun is in the 6th house, below 'the horizon'.

In the chart you've made, have a look and find which house the Sun is in and the interpretations below will give you their meaning.

Having your Sun in the 1st house has a different 'feel' to having your Sun in the 8th, and when you get a bit more into Astrology you'll discover so much more about that person.

The First House, House of Personality

I realised I had everything to win and nothing to lose.
Gene Wilder

This location is when the person was born at dawn, just as the Sun was rising, so consequently they will be good at initiating and starting projects and ideas. They tend to be a little like the first sign of the Zodiac, Aries: more forceful, more confident and more assertive. They also work quicker than other placements and can get a job done in less time than others.

The Second House, House of Money, Material Possessions and Self-Worth

The dancer's body is simply the luminous manifestation of the soul.
Isadora Duncan

This is the house that represents the things that we own. The practical world. Energy will be spent on accumulating possessions or financial security. Enjoyment will be found from holding, touching, truly experiencing things… tactile experiences like massage are generally treasured. All the senses need to be fulfilled and food is not a necessity, it can be a joy.

The Third House, House of Communication & Short Journeys

I started writing at school. I was always top of my class in composition, essays, English Lit and all of that.
Joan Collins

Like the third *sign* Gemini, the third house wants to engage with others by communicating with them. They would need a mobile phone, access to letters, telephones, conversations and all forms of communication. Being able to chat or write satisfies this house. As it also governs short journeys, having some means of transport is good.

The Fourth House, House of Home, Family & Roots

Family is not an important thing, it's everything.
Michael J. Fox

This is where the home becomes important. 'Family' in all its varied combinations will be a high priority. Cooking, snuggling up to others, pets, being close to significant others and the domestic world are all important. Children with this placement love to be home educated, but whatever they do stick the word 'home' in front of it and you'll succeed.

The Fifth House, House of Creativity & Romance

I was an art student at the time, like thousands of others.
Ray Davies

The fifth house is concerned with being able to shine. Being the centre of attention is also a plus. Red carpets, heaps of praise and appreciative recognition keep this combination happy. Creativity, drama, having lots of children or being with children, or creating or acting or being artistic are all expressed with the Sun here.

The Sixth House, House of Work & Health

When I repress my emotion my stomach keeps score.
Enoch Powell

The sixth house has its focus on everything related to health. It also is the work that we do. The Gemini Sun here will want to be well, healthy and organised. It's not unheard of for them to work in the health and healing sector or at least be concerned about their own and others' health issues. Good at detail and intricate tasks.

The Seventh House, House of Relationships & Marriage

I married the first man I ever kissed. When I tell this to my children, they just about throw up.
Barbara Bush

The Gemini Sun here will want to share their life with a significant other. Being single won't wash. Until their close personal relationship is organised life feels bleak. When attached to a 'Significant Other', life has new meaning. When they find that true love, their life seems complete and they can spread love and warmth around them.

The Eighth House, House of Life Force in Birth, Sex, Death & After-Life

They declaim against the passions without bothering to think that it is from their flame philosophy lights its torch.
Marquis de Sade

The intensity of the eighth house with the Gemini Sun makes an individual who is strong in character and un-swayed from their life's mission. Boredom is not on the menu! The ability to focus exclusively on one thing at a time can bring great results and if you add the word 'passion' in every now and then, they'll love you for it.

The Ninth House, House of Philosophy & Long Distance Travel

Have faith in your own thoughts.
Brooke Shields

Provided that the ninth house Sun in Gemini can philosophise about life's true meaning all is well. Foreign countries, long journeys, and an interest in other cultures will be expressed here. Keep passports at the ready, this is the Sun placement that loves to travel. Spirituality is never far away in all its guises and they love to feel the world is there to be explored.

The Tenth House, House of Social Identity & Career

People's behaviour makes sense if you think about it in terms of their goals, needs and motives.
Thomas Mann

You would expect this individual to be focused on their career and how they feel others perceive them. Being able to be recognised in their chosen field, no matter how long this may take, will guide them to success. They will work long hours, and over many years to get to the highest level of their life that they can, and they will focus on their career and work life.

The Eleventh House, House of Social Life & Friendships

When you work in TV, it's such a group effort, it's not about you.
Kylie Minogue

With the Gemini Sun in the 11th house individuals will want, no *need*: friends, groups, organizations, affiliations, societies that they can/will be members of. They don't see themselves in isolation to the world, they are part of it. Friendships are at the top of the list, so is charitable work and uniting the planet. They are happiest working or living with others.

The Twelfth House, House of Spirituality

The sight of the world, which was distraught with sorrow and which was eagerly asking for help and knowledge, did certainly affect my mind and cause me to understand that these psychic studies, which I had so long pursued, were of immense practical importance and could no longer be regarded as a mere intellectual hobby or fascinating pursuit of a novel research.
Sir Arthur Conan Doyle

We cast away priceless time in dreams, born of imagination, fed upon illusion, and put to death by reality.
Judy Garland

I have noticed a lot of my clients who have Sun in the 12th really don't like living in the 'real world'. It all seems too painful and insensitive. The 12th house, like the sign Pisces, wants to merge with the fairies and angels and escape to Never-Never Land or at the very least, stay sleeping and dreaming for as long as possible. They feel better when they have somewhere to escape to emotionally, be that the beach, on a hilltop, or in a nice warm bath every now and then. They can also be fascinated by the occult or other forms of spirituality.

Chapter Six

The Problems

When someone's Moon comes under pressure (when they're under emotional pressure), all sorts of unhappy things can happen.

Sometimes my e-mails are from Indigos that are unhappy, maybe it's their job, or school or relationships that spark them off. I'll give you a short example of what happens astrologically.

This e-mail is from Billy, who lives in California in the USA. Like most Indigos, he's looking for 'validation' and for me to recognise he's an Indigo.

He's a Gemini, with Leo Ascendant and Moon in Aquarius.

I asked him what *exactly* was it that he wanted to know?

The truth, but in ways I already know the truth. Something is coming and many will be lost but the ones who are in the light will face grave opposition from those that have hidden in the dark. They will never be truly free and then be subjected for history to repeat. Remember those hidden in the dark were once upon the light.

We should have disarmed and learned the way of the light when offered but instead sacrificed our people for foreign technology with only evil intentions. I have been channelling Zadkiel* without ever knowing how to channel. In many ways he feels as if he's a part of me because I too have the undying urge to stop the hand.

Vague, I know this might be but obviously it's you who I'm supposed to meet. There are 12 others just like me, for in my dream my soul crossed over and I was told I'm seven of the thirteen.

I am technology inclined and my videos stopped working on my phone, and I've tried every fix imaginable and nothing works. So I started downloading videos and have finally seen your face.

*Zadkiel is the archangel of freedom, benevolence, mercy, and the Patron Angel of all who forgive.

First of all, we need to take into account the Ascendant, which in this case is Leo. I didn't ignore his e-mail, even though a number of other writers had. Generally speaking, unless you're used to people pouring their hearts out in e-mails, it can be quite an upsetting thing for the recipient; even though I'm more used to it now, it still can be distressing. I'm a mother don't forget, and I find it sad to see a young man or woman struggle with their spirituality.

Notice the different bits of his chart. I'll point them out.

The Gemini bit is the speed with which his e-mails came. This is his follow-up e-mail, but the first one was sent a few seconds after he found my e-mail address. Two seconds to be precise. Gemini wants swift 'contact'. If you text or e-mail a Gemini, they generally reply within 15 minutes or less, provided what you're telling them is *interesting*.

His concern is to find out 'the truth', but since everyone's truth is rather subjective I can't offer help with that one…

His Sun is in the 11th so groups and being with people is important; having some sort of altruistic purpose is also a concern. His Moon is in Aquarius, so he enjoys all the technology as Aquarius is happy with this.

Notice how he's talking in 'we' rather than 'I'… his concern is with the group, rather than the individual; again this is an Aquarian trait.

He also thinks he's part of a *special group* of 13 people (again the group) but to even think that is the Leo Ascendant thing, as in 'I'm special'.

After a few reassuring e-mails telling him not to worry and to find someone in the flesh who could help him, I didn't hear from him again.

My Gemini Wants to Move House, Change Location/Job, Change the Car/Kitchen/Bathroom Again!

This is, I'm afraid, part and parcel of being with a Gemini =

CHANGE. You will have to learn to live with it, or not 'be' with your Gemini. Change is like breathing to them. They might not be as changeable as they could be, and if they've got any planets in Taurus, then the changes might not happen as much or will be slower.

Try and find out WHY your Gemini wants to change things. It's generally because they're getting bored, and that's not a good place for a Gemini (see below).

If you don't want to move house or change location, at least allow them to make some changes *within* the house. A Gemini catchphrase could easily be 'Change is as good as a rest!'

Maybe they could paint a room a different colour. If they want to change their job, I'd let them as there is nothing worse than working in a job you don't like. It can be torture to an Air sign, as ideas and thoughts are important, and if they're stifled because of work pressures, they'll get ill.

Changing cars or moving things round in the home is no big deal. If your finances are separate, then you really can't tell them how to spend their money. If they have car problems, they can buy a new one or fix the old one. The communal areas of the house will only really need changing if they get out-dated or dull, but don't let them change areas of the home that are yours, like your office, if you don't want them to. As long as you explain your reasons, 99% of Geminis will be happy with your choices.

My Gemini Says I'm Getting Boring

There is a subtle difference between them accusing you of 'being boring' and them 'feeling bored'. Have a chat and find out which is the case here. If they're accusing you of being boring, then ask them what is it that they find boring? What would you need to 'do' or say to not be boring? If, which is more likely the case, they're feeling bored themselves, then they obviously need a challenge to feel complete. This is where the house moving/job changing thing comes in. While they're making those changes, they get their brains activated into thinking about different things. One of the worst scenarios for a Gemini is to eat the same food, see the same people, go to work on the same route; anything that has become 'samey' is likely to stifle their life force.

My Gemini Can't Make Up Their Mind About Me/It/This/That

Welcome to True Gemini Territory!

Both double-bodied signs (the other one is Pisces) and Libra do have difficulty making up their minds about things. This generally happens in a Gemini's case when they've been thinking too much.

You can get a Gemini to swear blind that their favourite colour is blue… then three weeks later they buy a pink dress/tie and you wonder what that big lecture they gave you was all about… One minute they might say they want to change their job, then five minutes later they're telling you how much they like their boss. Most Air signs tend to 'think aloud' by having discussions about 'stuff' as a way of filtering their best options out.

They might not always think these things, but if you consider how much they *do* think, the fact that they've changed their mind or not been able to make their mind up about something is only one part of their main personality.

In reality it doesn't really matter if they do or don't make up their minds, because, as we all know, actions speak louder than words. My aunt spent hours telling us how much weight she was going to lose, or how much she had lost, or what size clothes she was wearing… and no one was really bothered. She was the way she was, but she sort of shared this all with us, as she worked her way through what she might do, or not do, about it all. She never went on any sort of diet, or in fact took any extra exercise, or even ate less, so how she was going to reduce her weight, I'm not sure!

This is when writing things down helps the most. And they should NOT write using a computer. It doesn't work as well. If they need to make a choice about something, get them to write it all down on paper. The pluses and minuses. THEN they will see for themselves what they need to see, and everyone will be happier.

Chapter Seven

The Solutions

Now that you know a little bit about Astrology, how to make a chart and understand it, you're now fully equipped to identify a Gemini at 50 paces. In this chapter, we'll be learning how to help a Gemini that might have got bogged down into a negative space, might be struggling with some 'issue' or might have lost their sparkle.

When your Gemini hits that Bad Space, you will then need to tailor your help to account for their Ascendant or Moon sign.

When people are trying to cope with unexpected change or a dilemma, they generally respond better to treatment that is individual to their suffering. This is the basis of all Homeopathic prescribing.

Being individual.

And it will help your Gemini immensely for you to *listen to them!*

On the listening side, here's what Lauren tells us will help her:

As a Gemini I consider myself to be very good at communication. I can talk and I can listen, and I enjoy doing both.

Mostly, however, I find it is rare for another person to listen to me properly. I mean really listen, not just hear me. Because I'm good at small talk, subject discussions and intensive conversations (so long as they are not too boring), I assume that everyone else is too. But that is simply not the case. When I talk it's because I have something important to say; important to me. I expect other people to respect that; to listen and understand and converse back to me on that subject proving they have listened.

It's one thing to listen, as in having your ears open, your iPod turned off, facing the person who is speaking, not talking yourself. It's another thing to *truly* listen, and this is what you will have to do if they hit a hard patch.

True listening skills are this:

You need to reflect back to your Gemini what they said. So, if they tell you Jack has left home (again) and they're feeling sad and upset, you will have to ask something like:

What is it about Jack leaving this time that's the most upsetting?

You've mirrored back the problem and now you're asking for a specific reason for their upsetment. Is it because he said he's never coming back? (He said this last time.) Or is it because he's taken the car AND the keys to his office? Or is it something else?

Maybe this time he's also taken a case of clothes, which he's never done before, and his favourite picture that was in the hall.

It's the picture in the hall that's the most upsetting as it belonged to your grandmother who gave it to you both, not just him. So there will be a bit of anger mixed in there, with the shock and sadness.

Before you go any further, give your Gemini some of their Moon remedy. Or at the very least some Rescue Remedy and/or the Homeopathic remedy Ignatia. This is for emotional trauma.

That's easy enough, but what else can you 'do' to help when they've lost their job, or their partner's walked out, or a relative or friend has died?

Use one of the suggestions below that corresponds to your Gemini's birth chart.

If your brain isn't working, the best thing you can do is listen for a good hour, then suggest a complete change of scene. Geminis aren't very good at suffering for a long time; leave that to the Water signs: Cancer, Scorpio and Pisces.

Aries Asc or Moon

There is only one way to help this combo and that is to do something physical and/or sporty. Get on your running shoes or sports kit, and meet up with your Gemini and get them to thrash their feelings out on the tennis court, basketball court, football pitch, or anywhere that moves the body. If you want them to feel better, don't bother with conversation; ACTION is the needed solution. Try and avoid anything that might put you at risk. So don't arrange a fencing session or boxing match; you might find you're the target for any stressful feelings!

Taurus Asc or Moon

The energies with the Gemini/Taurus combination are aimed at wanting to feel safe and secure. Arrange a firm date and take your Gem/Tau to a good slap-up meal at a good well-stocked restaurant, or at the very least cook for them. Slow down and match their body language. Get the chocolates and good wine out, and ensure they're feeling relaxed. If you're any good at massage, you will be seen as their saviour, or hire someone qualified to smooth away those angsty energies with fragrant oils and soothing movements. The body needs to be attended to, so deep breathing and tactile contact is needed. The mind can be sorted out later.

Gemini Asc or Moon

Now you will have to have your wits about you and your ears peeled back. Pay attention to every word they say. A double Gemini needs to feel heard and understood. If you repeat back a summary of what they've told you, you're on solid ground. Maybe even get them to write down how they feel, as they'll be so speeding around with questions and remarks and jibes and damning one-liners, you might get singed in the process. When they've written as much as they can, change the subject and do something totally different like going for a walk or meeting up with some other friends.

Cancer Asc or Moon

A Gem/Can will want to *feel* their emotions. They will be overcome with them in fact, which might make them a little weepy. Get the tissues out and mirror their body language, and when they've cried their ocean, wrap them up in some soft, fluffy blanket and tuck them up on the sofa. Listen carefully to their words and look underneath what they're actually saying; tune into their feelings, which at this moment will be like the wave, overwhelming and wet. In a little while the wave will recede and they'll be back to normal. Hugs! Did I mention hugs? They will be needed in abundance when Gem/Can gets down, so snuggle up and embrace the hurt away.

Leo Asc or Moon

Do NOT ignore a Gem/Leo. They want to feel acknowledged and included. They will be running around, sighing and being dramatic and shouting, "Off With Their Heads!" or similar drastic cries. Ignore the drama but don't ignore the person. You could ask, "What will help you Now?" and do whatever they suggest, provided it's legal and do-able. Agree that life is unfair and lay out the red carpet of one-to-one special treatment with personal inclusion. Say their name more than once, in friendly tones. This always works a treat, and nod your head in agreement to their feelings, which by now will be buzzing around at an alarming rate. Get them to take one good, deep breath in... and slowly let it out and their sunny self will soon return.

Virgo Asc or Moon

With the Gem/Virgo person you will need to ooze calm and centredness. Remember the flower essence Centaury and administer 2 drops in water before you attempt any other form of help.

They need to switch their brains off for a while. Geminis have active, fast-moving brains anyway; couple that with Virgo's need for precision and all they can think about is how to *'make things perfect'* and will be striving to 'do' millions of things about it all. Worst-case scenario will see them like rabbits in the headlamps, frozen to one reoccurring idea which they find hard to break out of. Soothing music, Tai Chi, gentle body exercise, sensible food and lots of good sleep will bring them back to earth perfectly.

Libra Asc or Moon

Most Gemini/Libra combos will be worried about relationships… or 'The One'. If they've fallen out with their nearest and dearest you will find a weepy, questioning person needing careful handling. First of all, don't give them any choices. This is, after all, the person who will be deliberating a choice. Come or Go? Stay or Leave? Right or Wrong? Help the process by not giving them a choice and sweep them away to somewhere beautiful and presentable where they can experience a better balance of ideas. Don't correct them or get into an argument, don't talk too much, let the place you have chosen calm them enough to reconfigure and let them feel centred. Yoga, gentle massage, light, tuneful music, like Celtic harp or something equally soothing, will work well too.

Scorpio Asc or Moon

Stand Back! Don't get too close when Gem/Scorp lets rip. You will find them consumed with the passion of deep, excruciating, painful feelings and revenge might be on the agenda. Be aware that they will want to resolve whatever is going on with drastic, painful solutions. If you think about the colour of deep red blood you will get an idea of how they're feeling. It sucks! It's horrible! They want an END to it all (whatever is happening to them).

Get them to write the person or problem a letter. Tell them to put ALL their feelings into the writing… then make a bonfire or light a candle, and safely watch the pain and anguish be consumed by the flames. Be firm. Be 'there'. You can't do much other than wait out the feelings, which like all feelings will eventually subside.

Sagittarius Asc or Moon

To get a Gem/Sag to admit that there is a problem will be difficult. It's generally someone else that is the problem, so that will have to be the focus of the solution. Get some aged texts. The Bible or other friendly spiritual writings. A favourite guru or lama or other spiritual leader, and either lend or buy the book for them. Arrange a trip away to some far-off exotic land where they can 'escape' from the every-day-ness that has caused the problem. If finances are tight, get them to a local foreign restaurant or talk where the focus is on far-off and distant lands. They need to be surrounded by people and conversations that are different to their own, so they can feel free to have the thoughts/feelings and opinions they're having. If they enjoy sport, go to a game, anything that will be different to where they are at the moment. Change, exotic change is paramount.

Capricorn Asc or Moon

As Capricorn is ruled by Saturn and loves serious, sensible solutions, a Gem/Cap will want the advice and guidance from someone older and hopefully wiser than they are. Their main worry will be about 'the future' and they will be concerned that they've ruined their chances, or missed an opportunity. If you can find someone who has 'been there and done that' they will start to thaw a little. You could of course go one better and help them discover their ancestral line and research their family tree, as Cap/Gem loves that which is ancient and tried and tested. A short visit to a stately home or traditional concert might also help... and do NOT rush them to recover. They need time and space.

Aquarius Asc or Moon

If you can imagine the weirdest and wackiest solution to their problem, you will have found the elixir of happiness. Gem/Aqua loves that which can only be defined as 'unusual'. Stay away from mainstream ideas, go for that which is different and unregulated and you'll have the happiest Aqua/Gem on the planet. Staying up late discussing Life, the Universe and Everything will also go down well. You could take them out for a short trip to street entertainers, or meet with some art students or people co-creating an ecological event. You could plug them into a simulator so they can experience some wacky occurrence or play a computer game that doesn't have any set rules. Anything that is not normal, not regular, not earth-based. They want to feel connected to some life-changing human consciousness.

Pisces Asc or Moon

Get out your Angel cards, light the incense or some candles. Put on soft music, get away from 'life' and 'humans' and touch into the outer reaches of all that is cosmic and divine. Any form of divination will be welcomed. They will be worrying about their next life, and their Karma, so reassure them you've got that covered. The spiritual solution must be credible and not *too* fantastic or you'll lose them to the Gemini rationale. Keep their feet on the ground but let their mind go where nothing hurts and no one can intervene. Meditation, hypnotherapy, relaxation, angels, fairies, stone circles, making a pilgrimage – all will be welcome, and at the very least a long, fragrant bath with a big Do Not Disturb sign on the door!

Chapter Eight

Listening Tactics

Now that you have learned about the astrology of a Gemini, how to make and understand a chart, we're now going to go through the various permutations of Gemini-ness. The Gemini energy is slightly different when it's expressed 'as a child' to when it is 'as a boss', so here are the various scenarios that you might come across.

Your Gemini Child

If you are the parent to a Gemini child, you will learn very soon that you will have to answer, when they learn to speak, the eternal question: 'Why?'

This will happen every day, every moment of their waking life.

From the time you serve their *Rice Krispies*: *"Why do Rice Krispies crackle when you pour on the milk?"*

... to when you're getting them dressed to go out to play: *"Why do zips only go one way, Mummy, why can't they go backwards?"*

... to when they're having their lunch: *"Why must I eat my vegetables?"*

... to teatime: *"Why do hot drinks hurt your mouth?"*

... to bedtime when they ask: *"Why did Cinderella fall out with her sisters? I like my sisters."*...

If you can answer their questions, there will be other questions to replace them as Kotryna shares with us:

My mother said I was asking questions at such a speed she didn't have enough time to answer one and I'd ask another already... And then get back to the one I asked before, because I didn't get that answer.

So very early you will find it easier if you give them some good books or encyclopaedias or a laptop so they can Google or search the Internet to find out the answers themselves.

Again Kotryna sums this up nicely:

The best gift I got as a child from my parents was Children's Illustrated Encyclopedia. *I actually started reading it from page one as a normal book, and did leave my parents alone for a while. That's the best gift you can give to a Gemini child. (Or, nowadays, direct them to Google... But an actual book is better.)*

And it's no good when you say things like, *"Because it is"* or *"Because Mummy/Daddy says so"* as that will make them only ask, *"Why?"* again until you feel so exhausted you'd rather sit in the audience of a rock concert, with loud music blaring, so you can drown out that little voice piping up, *"Why?"*

They are *genuinely* interested, and to prevent them asking why is equivalent to telling an Aquarius not to have friends, or a Leo not to dance or a Taurus not to eat their dinner (!) or a Scorpio to tell you a secret.

Just don't go there.

Their little lives depend on being able to ask why. After a time they'll understand the answers they are given and will work out how to find them themselves by reading and asking *other* people questions, and you will cease to be the font-of-all-knowledge and at that point in time you might regret being so hasty to let that happen. You might even miss them asking you things.

One thing you will also have to learn is, how to listen. It will seem as if all that question asking means they just want to listen to you; but equally, underneath their barrage of queries is a small person wanting to connect, and their way to connect is by voice.

Kotryna tells us what it was like having a mother who never listened to her when she was little. Mum is a Taurus and far too practical to 'waste time' chatting:

She never listened to me. She would pretend she's listening while doing something else, but if asked for a reaction or to repeat what I just said, it was plain that she hadn't heard a word I said. When I confronted her about this, being older, she said I talked so much it was impossible to maintain attention so my talking somehow naturally became background noise. But I'd much easier take being told, "I am busy right now, maybe you could tell me later?" than becoming background noise. We don't talk for the sake of talking, we need someone who listens. Now that I think of it, it's what I'm always looking for in my life, in friends too – someone who would really listen. And I am a good listener myself, it's not a one-way street.

Queenie also has this to say about parenting a Gemini; being one herself she's more than qualified to make suggestions:

In regards to how Gemini children should be parented, talking and LISTENING to your children is at the top of the list. Do not dismiss them; we need communication. Being seen and not heard is not possible with us. Making Gemini children feel like what they have to say is important, and do not just humor them to get them to be quiet. They want to be heard.

They are intensely curious and want to try several different activities/hobbies, but parents should realize they may not stick with anything for any length of time. We like to dabble and sample, we like doing things with our hands. As a parent, don't discourage their changing interests, don't tell them they can't explore something because "you never finish anything". We have a need to experience a lot, just not too much in depth. We bore easily and can get into trouble if we can't find something to occupy ourselves easily. Luckily we are not difficult to entertain.

We also tend to like to do more than one thing at a time.

I personally function better with background noise – not complete silence. Your child may want to listen to music while reading or doing homework. It might not be possible to focus on only one thing at a time. Our minds tend to wander easily.

Make sure they have empathy and consideration for others' feelings. One thing about being a Gemini is that things roll off my back easily.

I'm not very sentimental or easily hurt, and I have a caustic sense of humor. I have to remind myself that other people's feelings are more easily hurt than mine, and other people may not get over things as quickly. Sensitivity is not my strong suit.

Don't let them procrastinate or avoid difficult issues; we tend to not want to deal with things painful or deep.

No one really likes to do things that are painful, but some people do enjoy their emotions and 'going deep'; so to give your Gemini child some experience in this area. I suggest a great book by a Libra gentleman Marshall Rosenberg called *Nonviolent Communication.*

As it's written by a Libra Air sign and one that Geminis get along with, you'll find his suggestions on how to voice difficult emotions without resorting to violence very empowering.

Your Gemini Boss

I have had a Gemini boss. He was the world's smoothest talker and used the word 'Passionate' so much I almost convinced myself that he was passionate about what he did.

He wasn't.

It was just his word for the moment… and it sounded good, so he used it.

He was extremely versatile. The business sold adult toys. Things like the 'Stomp Rocket' and Yo-Yos and skateboards. Originally the company sold kites and my boss expanded the range of goods they sold. He loved to do the talking to potential suppliers, and would get all excited when new products were launched.

He moved around the office and would never stay still in one place for more than half an hour, and loved to get into heated discussions (which he called meetings) with his business partner (Mr Sagittarius) about prices and colours and packaging and supplier contracts.

He was fun to work with but he was the eternal boy-child. He obviously never wanted to grow up and the business fed into his boyhood desires.

I had another boss who was Gemini and this one was female. She was the assistant manager of a store I worked in. She was friendly and loved going out so much she even came to a party at my house, though I barely knew her. She loved being in company, discussing whatever was the latest topic, and seemed never to be short of something to say. I found her easy to work for. She never insisted on anything other than a good working knowledge of the stock.

Your Gemini boss won't criticise you for tardiness, or office pranks, or talking in meetings; but she/he will mark you down if you don't know what you're on about, or you can't quote your stock levels or profit margins or your main competitors. You will get brownie points if you know good restaurants to eat in, good films you saw at the cinema, have a 'mate' who can fix things, do 'stuff' or 'sort out' things. If you have an accountant who can cook the books, even better! I'm not suggesting anything illegal, but someone who knows how to pay the least in tax will be welcomed with open arms.

If you laugh at his/her jokes, go out occasionally for an after-work drink, can flirt with suppliers or competitors you will be valued even more. Your skills will need to reflect those Gemini attributes, but don't become a twin; they'll soon detect you're only buttering them up and will drop you the next time promotions are considered.

Your Gemini boss will also want anything marked 'new' and will rejoice if any 'new' idea you come up with works, so treat your job as a place to stretch your mind.

Your Gemini (female) Lover

On the one hand your Gemini lover will want the relationship to progress swiftly; on the other they just seem happy flirting and talking about dating, not actually doing it.

Here's Lauren, a business banking consultant:

When I was young, flirting was a way of life. It was not something I learned or was taught. It came naturally. As I had average intelligence, average breeding and average looks then flirting gave me the edge I needed to interact with the opposite sex. It also covered up the fact that I was shy and lacking in confidence. All through my first marriage and up to my second, I used flirting as a tool to communicate, interact, influence and attract. When I met my second husband the flirting with men other than him stopped. I didn't need it anymore. However, I make a point to flirt with my husband at least once a day.

You will also have to lead the relationship. Obviously if they don't like something you're doing, they'll tell you, but a Gemini woman does much prefer to be led rather than to lead. You will also have to have a variety of things on your 'to do' list. It's no good taking them to the same restaurant all the time. They'll enjoy going to the cinema, theatre, concerts, gigs, anywhere that the 'view' is different. They love laughter and light entertainment, of any kind. They'll even be happy to stay in to watch a movie, as long, again, as it's interesting.

Here is a young lady called Amelia in London looking for a partner:

About me

Quirky, a bit weird, thoughtful and loves to laugh. And could beat you at Dr. Robotnik's Mean Bean Machine *with my eyes shut. Try if you dare!*

Who I'm looking for

If you like a good retro game, and a random conversation involving quotes from the original Total Recall, *and in fact any Arnie film, then I think we'll get on swimmingly. Also, if you find odd things funny, and can laugh no matter what.*

Relationship status

Single

Relationship sought

Let's see what happens; Long-term relationship; Short-term relationship

Has children?

No

Wants children?

Maybe

As you can tell from this little quote, she wants to be entertained. She's not going to want to make all the suggestions all the time, and one thing you'll have to accept very early is if she 'drops a hint' she means it. She *might* want to get married and she *might* want to have children, but she definitely will want entertaining and 'random conversation'.

Your Gemini (male) Lover

The same applies to Gemini men as it does to women. Keep changing the scenery, keep things moving, and don't stand still for long.

You will need some sort of transport, as 'going local' won't really appeal. You won't have to go far, but a few miles in the car will do the trick.

Here's Tom, a young man looking for love in London:

Hmmm, well, I just asked a 'friend' to describe me and he snatched the bottle of wine and Nurofen and ran off.

People tell me I'm funny though not sure if 'haha' or 'strange'.

Some say I'm pretty (Mum), some say I'm ugly (mates) so I suppose I'm pretty ugly.

I've always wanted a beard but it just gets too itchy. Will do it one day.

I only sing Johnny Cash in the shower, but anything by anybody, anywhere else.

I love scruffy, strange looking dogs but haven't got one... (yet). Cats do not do it for me.

I love a natter with an old lady.

I lie about how good a dancer I am when I've had a drink.

Haven't had a Curly Wurly for ages.

OK, OK, OK.

Above all there is nothing more valuable than a smile and I want to create and fill my life with as many smiles as possible with someone special. Right that's enough of that stuff.

Who I'm looking for

A positive person with a happy, caring nature and loads of love and laughter to give.

If you can get five chocolate digestives in your mouth and eat them without spilling any I would concede any of the above requests.

Again the description is very short. It's not very to the point, which shows he hasn't thought too deeply about what he wants his girlfriend to be like. At least Amelia describes what she's looking for as far as marriage and children are concerned. Tom hasn't mentioned any of that because it's not his priority. What is his priority is *living* life, rather than life passing by.

When I first started dating my Gemini ex-husband, he took me out to various restaurants. Each one had a 'story': he told me about the food, the place and the history. He took me to places where they served traditional East End of London food with pie and mash and something called eel liquor sauce because it is traditionally made using the water kept from the preparation of the stewed eels. The sauce has a green colour, from the parsley, and looked very strange! We also went to Jewish restaurants and had potato latkes: lovely potato pancakes; went to Indian restaurants and had onion bhajis. All this was very new to me as I'd not eaten out much, so my Gemini Moon found it very exciting and different.

This is the key to a Gemini man's heart: do something different, do it all day, everyday.

What to do if your Gemini relationship ends

As you have been dating a Gemini, you will need to explain why the relationship has ended as this young Gemini lady tells us:

> *If it wasn't the Gemini who ended the relationship, then they need a thorough explanation on WHY? Nothing is worse than a lifetime-long haunting 'why' you'll never get an answer to. We need to understand why.*

It doesn't have to be a complex explanation and even if it's just the standard: *"I've fallen out of love with you"*, make sure your Gemini is verbally told this. If you're too nervous to do that, at the very least write them a polite e-mail or letter. However, I do think if you've been dating someone, the very least you can do is tell them face-to-face. What's the worst that can happen? They might cry, they might be angry, they might be rude, but at least you've been honest and polite enough to prevent them from eternal questioning thoughts.

Fire Sign

If you are a Fire sign: Aries, Leo or Sagittarius, you will need something active and exciting to help you get over your relationship ending.

You will also need to use the element of Fire in your healing process.

Get a nice nightlight candle and light it and recite:

I… (your name) do let you… *(Gemini's name)* go, in the freedom and with love so that I am free to attract my true soul-love.

Leave the nightlight in a safe place to completely burn away. Allow at least an hour. In the meantime gather up any belongings or possessions that are your (now) ex-lover's and deliver them back to your Gemini. It's polite to telephone first and notify your ex when you will be arriving.

If you have any photos of you together or other mementos or even gifts, don't be in a rush to destroy them, as some Fire signs are prone to do. Better to put them away in a box in the attic or garage until you feel a little less upset.

In a few months' time go through the box and keep the things you like and give away the things you don't.

Earth Sign

If you are an Earth sign: Taurus or Virgo or Capricorn, you will feel less inclined to do something dramatic or outrageous. It might also take you slightly longer to recover your equilibrium, so allow yourself a few weeks and a maximum of three months to grieve.

You will be using the Earth element to help your healing with the use of some trusty crystals.

The best crystals to use are the ones associated with your Sun sign and also with protection.

Taurus = Emerald
Virgo = Agate
Capricorn = Onyx

Cleanse your crystal in fresh running water. Wrap it in some pretty silk fabric, then go on a walk into the countryside. When you find a suitable spot, that is quiet and where you won't be disturbed, dig a small hole and place your crystal in the ground.

Spend a few minutes thinking about your relationship, the good times and the bad. Forgive yourself for any mistakes you may have made.

Imagine a beautiful plant growing from the ground where you have buried your crystal, and the plant blossoming and growing strong.

This will represent your new love that will be with you when the time is right.

Air Sign

If you're an Air sign: our friend Gemini, Libra or Aquarius, you might want to talk about what happened first before you finish the relationship. Air signs need reasons and answers, and can waste precious life-energy looking for those answers. You might need to meet with your Gemini to tell him/her exactly what you think/thought about his/her opinions, ideas and thoughts. You might also be tempted to tell him/her what you think about them now, which I do not recommend.

Far better to put those thoughts into a tangible form by writing your ex-Gemini a letter.

It is not a letter that you are actually going to post, but you are going to put as much energy into it as if you were actually going to send it.

Write to them thus:

Dear Mr/Ms Gemini,
I expect you will be happy now in your new life, but there are a few
things I would like to know and understand before I say goodbye.

Then list all the annoying, aggravating, upsetting ideas that your (now) ex-Gemini indulged in. Make a list as long as you like. Put in as much detail as you feel comfortable with, including things like how many times they changed their mind, or told white lies, or said one thing and did another, or didn't answer any of your texts when you know if you don't answer theirs, they go ballistic...

Keep writing until you can write no more, then end your letter with something similar:

Even though we were not suited, and I suffered because of this, I wish you well on your path.

Or some other positive comment.

Then tear your letter into teeny little pieces and put them into a small container. We are now going to use the element of Air to rectify the situation.

Take a trip to somewhere windy and high, like the top of a hill, and when you're ready, open your container and sprinkle a few random pieces of your letter into the wind. Don't use the entire letter or you run the risk of littering, just enough pieces to be significant.

Watch those little pieces of paper fly into the distance and imagine them connecting with the nature spirits.

Your relationship has now ended.

Water Sign

If you are a Water sign: Cancer, Scorpio or Pisces, you might find it more difficult to recover quickly from your relationship. You might find yourself weeping at inopportune moments, or when you hear 'your' song on the radio, or when you see other couples happily being in each other's company. You might lie awake at night worrying that you have ruined your life and your ex-Gemini is having all the fun. As you might have gathered by now, this is unlikely. Your ex might be as upset as you.

Your emotional healing therefore needs to incorporate the Water element.

As you are capable of weeping for the World, the next time you are in floods of tears capture one small teardrop and place it into a small glass. Have one handy just for this purpose. Decorate it if you feel like it. Small flowers, stars, or twinkly things.

Now fill your glass to the top with tap water and place it on a table.

Then recite the following:

This loving relationship with you... (Gemini's name) has ended.
I reach out across time and space to you.
My tears will wash away the hurt I feel.
I release you from my heart, mind and soul.
We part in peace.

And then slowly drink the water. Imagine your hurt dissolving away, freeing you from all anxieties and releasing you from sadness.

Then spend the next few weeks being nice to yourself. If you need to talk, find someone you trust and confide in them. Keep tissues handy.

Your Gemini Friend

It isn't hard to be friends with a Gemini. They've probably got loads and loads of them anyway. Geminis attract friendships and connections like Velcro. Their friends will be divided into 'Work', 'Play', 'Family', 'Others'. You'll know which category you belong to, as your friends will all be mutual. It's rare for a Gemini to have a friend that doesn't also know another one of their friends.

Like other Air signs, you won't need to see them all the time, or be in their pocket. They prefer to connect lightly but frequently.

A bit like a butterfly going from flower to flower. I have never seen a butterfly stay very long in one place. Have you? They flit from here to there. They don't generally travel very long distances. Every now and then, they open and close their wings in the sunshine, and then they're off again from flower to flower. Think of this when you think of your Gemini friendship.

It needs to be varied and delicate.

If you do happen to hit a hard patch, your Gemini will be there to pull you through but they won't want constant reminders of those past troubles, so put them behind you and look to a rosier future.

As I mentioned earlier, my best friend is Gemini and we're linked with a Moon/Sun conjunction (Astrologuese for together in the same sign). Make your respective charts up and you'll soon find out how compatible you are, and also crucially, how much time you can spend together without falling out or getting bored.

One thing is for sure, if your Gemini hits a hard patch, you just 'being there' will be sufficient to calm their fears.

Kylie Minogue puts it brilliantly:

And when I go into a spin for no reason, when I feel totally clueless, I ask myself a thousand questions, who I am, what I want, where I'm going... He is there.

Your Gemini Mother

As I'm a Homeopath as well as an Astrologer I know a number of good Homeopathic authors and one of my favourites is Gemini Miranda Castro.

In her very helpful book *Mother and Baby* she tells us what it was like becoming a mother for the first time.

I became happily pregnant in 1978, and I loved it. I loved the feeling of a life taking shape inside me, of his swimmings and turnings. I loved the shape my body took, my big, soft roundness... I was irrationally scared my baby would be stillborn... to feelings, still unresolved from an abortion I had had the year before... My labour was long, hindered by my fear and anxiety and because I wasn't allowed to eat...

Motherhood was a huge shock, an explosion of mixed emotions. I had so much to adapt to, seemingly so quickly, that I found myself frequently chasing my own tail as I struggled to understand what to do next! I wish I had known it would be such hard work.[14]

The reason I have included this extract is because of the last line: *"I wish I had known it would be such hard work."*

If you remember at the beginning of this book, I told you how my ex-husband liked to know the worst-case scenario. I think Gemini is the only sign this will relate to. They want to know the good and the bad. Unlike a Leo who only wants to know the good. Or a Capricorn who always fears the worst anyway.

A Gemini mother will feel happier if she knows *everything* that can go wrong, or happen, as well as all the positive things she can focus on. So if you have a Gemini friend who is going to give birth for the first time, get them to read Miranda's book or at the very least, explain what *could* go wrong, what *might* happen, and what is *the best* that can happen.

My lovely auntie, who recorded my birth data in her Ephemeris, was also a Gemini and so was my lovely grandmother, so I've had first-hand experience of being with Gemini mothers. I also know a number of mums my age who are Geminis so it's a subject I know well.

First of all, your Gemini mother needs something to keep her brain active. If all she is doing is domestic tasks without any form of mental stimulation, you're going to have a very grumpy Gemini mother.

I know a number of journalists and writers who are Gemini. I know if they work too much they miss their kids, but equally if they don't work at all they get a bit tired and unhappy.

My grandmother never worked a day in her life, but she was a very industrious person, always knitting or sewing or playing the piano.

My mother wrote about her in her book *Pompey Roots*:

> One thing I specially remember about my Mother were her endless 'sayings'. She had one for every occasion:
>
> The better the day, the better the deed.
>
> If you want a job done properly, do it yourself.
>
> You've got to eat a peck of dirt before you die.
>
> You'd lose your head if it wasn't screwed on.
>
> One on and one off and one in the wash.
>
> In and out like a cat in a tripe shop.[15]

Both my maternal grandmother and paternal auntie loved to chat. They were never happier than having someone to have a 'good' conversation with. And unlike a Leo, the conversation didn't have to be about them, or even anything they were interested in. As long as the conversation flowed and there was 'something to say', they were happy. I even interviewed my grandmother when she was very elderly with my little tape recorder and she told me the (true) story about *'How Grandpa Latham Shot a Russian in the 1st World War'*.

Motherhood itself isn't necessarily appealing to a Gemini; what is appealing is helping their children learn things. Gemini mothers love to pass on information.

Brigida lived in East Timor/Timor-Leste, an island off the coast of Indonesia. She tells us about her Sun Gemini, Moon Sagittarius mother who was first in an arranged marriage at age eleven. When she was sixteen, she had her first baby who sadly died. She eventually gave birth to six children, after losing another child.

My mother paid attention to the little things in our life. She always tried to make our birthdays special every year. She also sewed our clothing herself, including shirts for my father and my two brothers. Our house in Uato-Carbau was always crowded, because other parents wanted their kids to learn sewing, embroidery and cooking from my mother.

My mother always reminded us of the importance of education. She did not want us to follow her path. My parents never differentiated between their sons and daughters. They sent all of us to elementary school in Ossu. My eldest sister and I went to the nuns' boarding school and my brothers went to a male boarding school. My mother was very supportive of us girls. Often, during my father's absences, she reminded us to study hard as she believed that only with good educations could our lives get better.

Brigida tells us more about that natural Gemini spirit:

She made friends with everyone. When I was little, there was a traditional market every Sunday after prayer. My mother would always prepare a meal that was more than what her family needed. Then she sat in front of our house, waiting for people to return from market. She would invite them in and offer them lunch or cups of coffee or tea. If they weren't hungry or thirsty, she would sit and chew a bittle-nut with them.[16]

Now, if you change that account slightly and add 'tea and cakes' instead of the meal, that could be anywhere in the UK. In the USA change tea for coffee and cookies, and again the story would still be the same. The key point is: *"She made friends with everyone."* This is a natural Gemini trait, and one, if your mother is Gemini, you will have to recognize and encourage.

Your Gemini Father

Your Gemini father will be a mix of different, interesting

energies. He will be happy and full of life one day, questioning 'Life, the Universe and Everything' the next. He will have a large circle of friends, some from work, some from his hobbies and like most Geminis he will keep them separate.

Manuka tells us about her Gemini father:

My late father was a Gemini. He was born in the Ukraine, right on the present day border with Poland; his family spent the first few years of his life moving about as itinerant farmers (and his mother was a midwife). When WWII ended, they lived in a refugee camp, and eventually migrated to the United States. He was an eloquent character, and generous and open-minded. I often say that my father was willing to give me anything in the world except a straight answer.

My father was a compulsive talker. When my sisters and I were young, he would often take us to a doughnut shop or a diner, and sit and talk for hours. Sometimes it was even hard for me to get a word in edgewise. He also enjoyed talking on the phone, and could converse for hours that way as well. And he was never shy about dashing off a letter; he loved sending and receiving mail, as he worked for the post office.

He worked for the US Postal Service for 30+ years. However, he applied for route changes frequently, every couple of years. By the end of his working years, he had probably delivered the mail to every house in town. During the six years that he lived on his own, he moved from apartment to apartment (about seven times).

His favorite school subjects were literature and philosophy (he was an ardent fan of Tolstoy). His hobbies were reading, drawing, and 'people-watching'. He could spend a whole day in a diner, talking with the waitresses and striking up conversations with interesting strangers.

He spoke several languages: Polish, Russian, and German in his childhood, English after emigrating to the United States, and a smattering of Spanish after marrying my mother (who is of

Mexican-American descent).

Perhaps ironically for such an avid talker, he loved silent film comedians. Charlie Chaplin, Buster Keaton, Harold Lloyd, Laurel and Hardy. He also enjoyed Groucho Marx and Bob Hope.

This is a Sun Gemini, Moon Sagittarius person and notice how he changed his *route* at work, rather than the job itself. He enjoyed conversation, could speak more than one language, loved reading and 'people watching'. All typical Gemini traits. If your father is a Gemini, provided your charts don't clash, you should have a parent that is very happy to pass on his skills and hobbies to you. The only problem occurs if your hobbies clash. I know a Taurus whose father was Gemini and their point of interest was watercolours and painting, but his dad also liked to pigeon race, and the son wasn't that interested in it. When his father retired, he spent a lot of his time in his pigeon loft and out with the birds, racing them, which wasn't really something they could 'share'.

Your interests do have to be similar, or there might be a clash. If that's the case, just agree to disagree; but at the very least, let your father tell you about his hobbies and listen!

Your Gemini Sibling

If your sibling is a Gemini, it will help to work out what Element you are. If you're either an Air or Fire sign, things should work out reasonably well. You might bicker, you might argue, you might disagree on a number of issues, but underneath there will be the sparkling understanding that these Elements have with each other.

Sarah is an Aries and has this to say about her Gemini sister:

I have a sister who is a Gemini. I'm not sure I'd call her logical. We all do at times think she is nuts—but that is another story! She is however, a very intelligent woman. Always was. It almost seems like it comes natural to her and it surprises me in a way because she is not & was not ever a reader - save romance novels - and yet she has/had this knack of being able to do well in every subject.

If you're a Water or Earth sign, your Gemini brother or sister might drive you crazy.

Earth signs especially find it hard to get on with their Air sign brethren. This is because one is motivated by hard, real, tangible facts and things, and the other by rapidly changing ideas, thoughts and changeable feelings. This drives Earth signs wild and, unless you have complementary Moon signs or Ascendants, might cause eons of grief.

It would help to make both of your charts and study them carefully, and find some point of similarity. Maybe you both have Venus in the same sign or Element. Maybe your Moons get on, or your Mars. Unfortunately there isn't room in this little book to give you every possible combination but suffice to say that if you look carefully you'll find something to agree on, even if it's your Plutos (which takes the longest time to change sign).

Do expect your Gemini sibling to be one thing one day, and something else the next. If you prepare yourself mentally for their changeability and don't expect them to be like you, you won't be disappointed.

I hope you have enjoyed reading a little about the Sun sign Gemini and are now a little more confident about making an Astrological birth chart. If we all understood each other a little better, the world would be even more lovely to live in.

I wish you well in your life, and I am sending peace and happiness to you.

References

1. *The Astrologers and Their Creed*, Christopher McIntosh, 1971, Arrow Books Ltd, imprint of the Hutchinson Group, London

2. p. 70, *The Dawn of Astrology: A Cultural History of Western Astrology, The Ancient and Classical Worlds*, Nicholas Campion, 2008, Hambledon Continuum, London SE1

3. *The Handbook of Astronomy*, Clare Gibson, 2009, Kerswell Books Ltd

4. *Essentials Astronomy: A Beginner's Guide to the Sky at Night*, Paul Sutherland, 2007, Igloo Books Ltd, Sywell

5. *Astrological Counselling, A basic guide to astrological themes in person to person relationships*, Christine Rose, 1982, The Aquarian Press, Northamptonshire.

6. *Retrograde Planets: Traversing the Inner Landscape,* Erin Sullivan 1992, Arkana, Penguin Books Ltd, 27 Wrights Lane, London W8 5TZ, England

7. *Astrology for Dummies,* Rae Orion, 1999, IDG Books Worldwide, Inc, Foster City, CA 94404

8. *Astrology. The Stars and Human Life: A Modern Guide*, Christopher McIntosh, 1970, Macdonald Unit 75, London

9. *Linda Goodman's Love Signs, A New Approach to The Human Heart*, 1980, Pan Books Ltd, London SW10

10. *Easy Astrology Guide: How to Read Your Horoscope*, Maritha

Pottenger, 1996, ACS Publications Inc., US

11. *The Instant Astrologer*, Felix Lyle, Bryan Aspland, 1998, Piatkus Books, London W1

12. http://www.telegraph.co.uk/culture/5421264/Hugh-Laurie-interview.html

13. The New Waite's Compendium of Natal Astrology, 1967, Routledge and Kegan Paul Ltd, London

14. *Miranda Castro's Homeopathic Guides, Mother and Baby, Pregnancy, Birth and your baby's first year*, 1992, Pan Books, London SW1

15. *Pompey Roots, A History of the Latham/Lonnon Families, Jean English*, self-published, www.jeanenglish.co.uk

16. http://mymothersstory.org/2012/06/brigida-silvas-story-of-etelvina/#more-1616

Further Information

The Astrological Association
   www.astrologicalassociation.com

The Bach Centre, The Dr Edward Bach Centre, Mount Vernon,
Bakers Lane, Brightwell-cum-Sotwell, Oxon, OX10 0PZ, UK
   www.bachcentre.com

Astrological Chart Information

Chart information and birth data from astro-databank at www.astro.com and www.astrotheme.com.

No accurate birth data
Aung San Suu Kyi, 19th June 1945, Rangoon (Yangon), Burma

Helena Bonham Carter, 26th May 1966, Golders Green, London, UK, Moon Leo

Che Guevara, 14th May 1928, Rosario (Santa Fe), Argentina, Sun Gemini, Moon Pisces

Ascendant
Isadora Duncan, 26th May 1877, San Francisco, CA, USA, 2.10am, Aries Ascendant, Sun in 2nd, Moon Scorpio

Les Paul (Lester William Polsfuss), 9th June 1915, Waukesha, WI, USA, 2am, Taurus Ascendant, Sun in 2nd, Moon Taurus

Angelina Jolie, 4th June 1975, Los Angeles, CA, USA, 9.09am, Cancer Ascendant, Sun in 11th, Moon Aries

Queen Victoria, 24th May 1819, London, England, UK, 4.15am, Gemini Ascendant, Sun in 1st, Moon Gemini

Anne Frank, 12th June 1929, Frankfurt am Main, Germany, 7.30am, Leo Ascendant, Sun in 11th, Moon Leo

Igor Stravinsky, 17th June 1882, Oranienbaum, Russia, 12pm, Virgo Ascendant, Sun in 10th, Moon Cancer

Paula Abdul, 19th June 1962, Los Angeles, CA, USA, 2.32pm, Libra Ascendant, Sun in 9th, Moon Capricorn

Nicole Kidman, 20th June 1967, Honolulu, HI, USA, 3.15pm, Scorpio Ascendant, Sun in 8th, Moon Sagittarius

Bob Dylan, 24th May 1941, Duluth, MN, USA, 9.05pm, Sagittarius Ascendant, Sun in 6th, Moon Taurus

Brooke Shields, 31st May 1965, Manhattan, NY, USA, 1.45pm, Virgo Ascendant, Sun in 9th, Moon Gemini

Naomi Campbell, 22nd May 1970, Westminster, London, UK, 1am, Capricorn Ascendant, Sun in 5th, Moon Sagittarius

Ray Davies, 21st June 1944, Fortis Green, England, UK, 00.20am, Aquarius Ascendant, Sun in 5th, Moon Cancer

Paul McCartney, 18th June 1942, Liverpool, England, UK, 2am, Pisces Ascendant, Sun in 4th, Moon Leo

Moon

Jackie Stewart, 11th June 1939, Dumbuck, Scotland, UK, 2.50pm, Libra Ascendant, Sun in 9th, Moon Aries

Joan Collins, 23rd May 1933, Paddington, London, UK, 3am, Aries Ascendant, Sun in 3rd, Moon Taurus

Tom Jones, 7th June 1940, Pontypridd, Wales, UK, 00.10am, Capricorn Ascendant, Sun in 5th, Moon Gemini

Kylie Minogue, 28th May 1968, Melbourne, Australia, 11am, Cancer Ascendant, Sun in 11th, Moon Gemini

Bob Hope, 29th May 1903, Eltham, England, UK, Libra Ascendant, Sun in 8th, Moon Cancer

Ian McKellen, 25th May 1939, Burnley, England, UK, 9.30pm, Sagittarius Ascendant, Sun in 6th, Moon Virgo

Clint Eastwood, 31st May 1930, San Francisco, CA, USA, 5.35pm, Scorpio Ascendant, Sun in 7th, Moon Leo

Sandra Bernhard, 6th June 1955, Flint, MI, USA, 9am, Leo Ascendant, Sun in 11th, Moon Sagittarius

Priscilla Presley, 24th May 1945, Brooklyn (Kings County), NY, USA, 10.40pm, Capricorn Ascendant, Sun in 11th, Moon Scorpio

Marilyn Monroe, 1st June 1926, Los Angeles, CA, USA, 9.30am, Leo Ascendant, Sun in 10th, Moon Aquarius

Johnny Depp, 9th June 1963, Owensboro, KY, USA, Leo Ascendant, Sun in 11th, Moon Capricorn

Allen Ginsberg, 3rd June 1926, Newark, NJ, USA, 2am, Pisces Ascendant, Sun in 4th, Moon Pisces

Houses

Gene Wilder, 11th June 1933, Milwaukee, WI, USA, 3.50am, Gemini Ascendant, Sun in 1st, Moon Aquarius

Michael J. Fox, 9th June 1961, Edmonton, AB, Canada, 00.15am, Aquarius Ascendant, Sun in 4th, Moon Taurus

Ray Davies, 21st June 1944, Fortis Green, England, UK, 00.20am, Aquarius Ascendant, Sun in 5th, Moon Cancer

Enoch Powell, 16th June 1912, Birmingham, England, UK, 9.50pm, Capricorn Ascendant, Sun in 6th, Moon Cancer

Barbara Bush, 8th June 1925, Rye, NY, USA, 7pm, Sagittarius Ascendant, Sun in 7th, Moon Capricorn

Marquis de Sade, 2nd June 1740, Paris, France, 5pm, Scorpio Ascendant, Sun in 8th, Moon Virgo

Thomas Mann, 6th June 1875, Lübeck, Germany, 10.15am, Virgo Ascendant, Sun in 10th, Moon Cancer

Judy Garland, 10th June 1922, Grand Rapids, MN, USA, 6am, Cancer Ascendant, Sun in 12th, Moon Sagittarius

Sir Arthur Conan Doyle, 22nd May 1859, Edinburgh, Scotland, UK, 4.55am, Gemini Ascendant, Sun in 12th, Moon Aquarius

Dodona Books offers a broad spectrum of divination systems to suit all, including Astrology, Tarot, Runes, Ogham, Palmistry, Dream Interpretation, Scrying, Dowsing, I Ching, Numerology, Angels and Faeries, Tasseomancy and Introspection.

9781782790990